Gun Control

OPPOSING
VIEWPOINTS®
DIGESTS

**BOOKS IN THE
OPPOSING VIEWPOINTS DIGESTS SERIES:**

Abortion

The American Revolution

Animal Rights

The Bill of Rights

Biomedical Ethics

Child Abuse

The Civil War

The Death Penalty

Drugs and Sports

Endangered Species

The Environment

The Fall of the Roman Empire

Gangs

The Great Depression

Gun Control

The 1960s

Slavery

Teen Violence

Gun Control

TERRY O'NEILL

$$\left[\begin{array}{c} \textbf{OPPOSING} \\ \textbf{VIEWPOINTS}^{®} \\ \textbf{DIGESTS} \end{array}\right]$$

Greenhaven Press, Inc., San Diego, California

Library of Congress Cataloging-in-Publication Data

O'Neill, Terry, 1944–
    Gun control / Terry O'Neill.
      p. cm. — (Opposing viewpoints digests)
    Includes bibliographical references and index.
    Summary: Presents opposing arguments on gun control, including gun availability and its influence on society, the constitutionality of gun control, effective measures in reducing gun violence, and the effects of a gun ban on society.
      ISBN 1-56510-879-5 (lib. : alk. paper) — ISBN 1-56510-878-7 (pbk. : alk. paper)
    1. Gun control—United States—Juvenile literature 2. Firearms ownership—Government policy—United States—Juvenile literature. 3. Firearms—Law and legislation—United States—Juvenile literature. [1. Gun control. 2. Firearms ownership. 3. Firearms—Law and legislation.] I. Title II. Series.
    HV7436.O54 2000
    363.3'3'0973—dc21   99-048707
                                                                              CIP

Cover Photo: A Wiener/Gamma-Liason
American Heritage Center, University of Wyoming 82
The Denver Public Library/Western History Collection 11, 87
MOD Pattern Room, Nottingham 69
PhotoDisc 15
Simon Wiesenthal Center Archives 47

©2000 by Greenhaven Press, Inc.
PO Box 289009, San Diego, CA 92198-9009

Printed in the U.S.A.

CONTENTS

Foreword   7

Introduction: A Brief History of Gun Control   9

Chapter 1: How Does Gun Availability Affect Society?

1. Gun Availability Contributes to Crime and Violence   22

2. Gun Ownership Protects People from Crime and
    Violence   26

3. School Violence Is Caused by Gun Availability   31

4. School Violence Is Not Caused by Gun Availability   37

Chapter 2: Is Gun Control Constitutional?

1. Gun Ownership Is Protected by the Second
    Amendment   43

2. Gun Ownership Is Not Protected by the Second
    Amendment   49

**Chapter 3: What Measures Would Be Effective in
Reducing Gun Violence?**

1. The Government Should Pass Stronger
    Gun-Control Laws   55

2. Existing Gun-Control Laws Should Be More Strongly
    Enforced   61

3. Gun Manufacturers Should Be Held Responsible for
    Gun Violence   67

4. Gun Manufacturers Should Not Be Held Responsible
    for Gun Violence   73

Chapter 4: How Would a Gun Ban Affect Society?

1. Banning Guns Would Harm Society   80

2. Banning Guns Would Not Solve America's Problem
    with Violence   85

3. Banning Guns Would Help Reduce the Level of
    Violence in Society   91

Study Questions   97
Appendix A: Facts About Gun Control   99
Appendix B: Excerpts from Related Documents   104
Organizations to Contact   115
For Further Reading   121
Works Consulted   127
Index   137
About the Author   144

FOREWORD

The only way in which a human being can make some approach to knowing the whole of a subject is by hearing what can be said about it by persons of every variety of opinion and studying all modes in which it can be looked at by every character of mind. No wise man ever acquired his wisdom in any mode but this.

—John Stuart Mill

Today, young adults are inundated with a wide variety of points of view on an equally wide spectrum of subjects. Often overshadowing traditional books and newspapers as forums for these views are a host of broadcast, print, and electronic media, including television news and entertainment programs, talk shows, and commercials; radio talk shows and call-in lines; movies, home videos, and compact discs; magazines and supermarket tabloids; and the increasingly popular and influential Internet.

For teenagers, this multiplicity of sources, ideas, and opinions can be both positive and negative. On the one hand, a wealth of useful, interesting, and enlightening information is readily available virtually at their fingertips, underscoring the need for teens to recognize and consider a wide range of views besides their own. As Mark Twain put it, "It were not best that we should all think alike; it is difference of opinion that makes horse races." On the other hand, the range of opinions on a given subject is often too wide to absorb and analyze easily. Trying to keep up with, sort out, and form personal opinions from such a barrage can be daunting for anyone, let alone young people who have not yet acquired effective critical judgment skills.

Moreover, to the task of evaluating this assortment of impersonal information, many teenagers bring firsthand experience of serious and emotionally charged social and health problems, including divorce, family violence, alcoholism and drug abuse, rape, unwanted pregnancy, the spread of AIDS, and eating disorders. Teens are often forced to deal with these problems before they are capable of objective opinion based on reason and judgment. All too often, teens' response to these deep personal issues is impulsive rather than carefully considered.

Greenhaven Press's Opposing Viewpoints Digests are designed to aid in examining important current issues in a way that develops critical thinking and evaluating skills. Each book presents thought-provoking argument and stimulating debate on a single issue. By examining an issue from many different points of view, readers come to realize its complexity and acknowledge the validity of opposing opinions. This insight is especially helpful in writing reports, research papers, and persuasive essays, when students must competently address common objections and controversies related to their topic. In addition, examination of the diverse mix of opinions in each volume challenges readers to question their own strongly held opinions and assumptions. While the point of such examination is not to change readers' minds, examining views that oppose their own will certainly deepen their own knowledge of the issue and help them realize exactly why they hold the opinion they do.

The Opposing Viewpoints Digests offer a number of unique features that sharpen young readers' critical thinking and reading skills. To assure an appropriate and consistent reading level for young adults, all essays in each volume are written by a single author. Each essay heavily quotes readable primary sources that are fully cited to allow for further research and documentation. Thus, primary sources are introduced in a context to enhance comprehension.

In addition, each volume includes extensive research tools. A section containing relevant source material includes interviews, excerpts from original research, and the opinions of prominent spokespersons. A "facts about" section allows students to peruse relevant facts and statistics; these statistics are also fully cited, allowing students to question and analyze the credibility of the source. Two bibliographies, one for young adults and one listing the author's sources, are also included; both are annotated to guide student research. Finally, a comprehensive index allows students to scan and locate content efficiently.

Greenhaven's Opposing Viewpoints Digests, like Greenhaven's higher level and critically acclaimed Opposing Viewpoints Series, have been developed around the concept that an awareness and appreciation for the complexity of seemingly simple issues is particularly important in a democratic society. In a democracy, the common good is often, and very appropriately, decided by open debate of widely varying views. As one of our democracy's greatest advocates, Thomas Jefferson, observed, "Difference of opinion leads to inquiry, and inquiry to truth." It is to this principle that Opposing Viewpoints Digests are dedicated.

A Brief History of Gun Control

"Gun control has been around since the beginning of firearms," said reporter Eric Westervelt on a radio program on gun control. He pointed out that "who could bear arms and where was restricted in Colonial times. And later, in some frontier towns, guns had to be placed in a secure hold or left at the town line."[1]

Although gun control has a long history, it did not become an issue of significant national controversy until recent times. Today, gun control often inspires heated discussions and obstinate refusals to listen to opposing views. The issue tends to be a very personal one, often inspired by experience. Many people who grew up in a hunting culture, for example, or who have spent time in the military, resolutely hang onto the right of individuals to own guns. Likewise, many people who have had an unpleasant experience involving gun crime or violence are adamant that guns must be controlled much more strongly than they are today, or even banned altogether.

High-profile crimes such as school shootings and the tragically large numbers of gun deaths among minority youth have raised many people's awareness about guns and sparked renewed debate about gun control. Strident speeches and press releases from organizations on both sides of the issue have also contributed to the controversy. Private groups as well as government bodies hold many lively debates on what forms of gun control, if any, should be enacted, and both individuals and organizations exert strong pressure on lawmakers to enact or oppose gun-control laws.

To put the issue in perspective, here is a brief history of guns and gun control in America.

Guns in Early America

Guns were a vital part of the birth of the United States. Historian James B. Tefethan writes, "Freedom from Great Britain was . . . won by ordinary citizens whose will to fight for liberty was backed by an intimate knowledge of firearms gained through the use of personal weapons."[2] From the time they started settling in America, the colonists used firearms to put meat on the table, to provide protection against mauraders, and to tame the Western frontier. And after the colonists' superior shooting ability and novel, guerrilla fighting style beat the British, the colonists wanted to guarantee that they would never again have to fear a tyrannical government. Part of their insurance was the Second Amendment to the Constitution.

Ratified in 1791, three and a half years after the Constitution, the Second Amendment is part of the Bill of Rights. The amendment states, "A well regulated Militia, being necessary to the security of a free State, the right of the people to keep and bear Arms, shall not be infringed." The exact intent of this amendment is still debated today, but it clearly promises that firearms will be available in some way to some people.

Yet despite the Second Amendment, not everyone was allowed to "keep and bear arms." Some of the earliest firearm restrictions were state and local laws enacted to prevent blacks from having guns. Just as they were denied other freedoms, blacks in America—whether freemen or slaves—were forbidden to possess firearms in many parts of the country.

Early American history is filled with conflict. Quickly following the Revolutionary War came the War of 1812, the Indian wars, the westward movement, and the Civil War, all of which kept American firearms blazing and people clinging tenaciously to their ever-improving guns. The extremely accurate Pennsylvania rifle helped ensure an American victory against the British, and the tiny, easily concealed Derringer, invented in the 1830s, accompanied many an Eastern gentleman and Western gambler on their daily rounds. And, of course, the Winchester rifle and Colt six-shooter were the tools of choice for many of those who aimed to tame the frontier, which often involved fighting natives, fighting one another for the rights to land and resources, and hunting animals for food and profit.

BUFFALO BILL'S WILD WEST.
CONGRESS, ROUGH RIDERS OF THE WORLD.

MISS ANNIE OAKLEY,
THE PEERLESS LADY WING-SHOT.

The gunslingers of the Wild West, such as Annie Oakley (pictured), were portrayed as romantic heroes.

The era of the Wild West did not end until the beginning of the twentieth century, and, before it was over, it had inspired a whole new kind of entertainment: exciting Wild West shows and penny novels about gunslinging villains and heroes. These did not show the toil, sweat, and losses suffered by the majority of those who "conquered" the West. Instead, they portrayed the gunslinger as a kind of romantic folk hero—courageous, independent, and with an unbreakable code of honor. By examining our popular entertainment today, we can see how this glamorized image of the man with a gun has remained with us.

Gangs and Gangsters

In 1919 a strong temperance movement led to the addition of the Eighteenth Amendment to the Constitution. It banned liquor in the United States. This began the Prohibition era, also called the Roaring Twenties. Quite contrary to its proponents' intent, Prohibition gave rise to a huge growth of gang-sterism and crime that did not end when the amendment was repealed in 1933. Making, importing, and distributing liquor became a major business operated by criminals who used guns to safeguard themselves and their business against law enforcement officials and against each other. They had many highly publicized gun battles and ambushes, shooting hun-dreds of rounds of ammunition at each other in a single skir-mish. One of the gangsters' favored weapons was the "tommy gun," the Thompson submachine gun that American troops had used during World War I. Another was the sawed-off shotgun. These weapons eventually became the target of the nation's first federal gun-control laws.

The gangsters' crimes did not only affect other gangsters. As with acts of violence in today's society, many innocent bystanders were shot and killed. Outraged voters put pressure on the government to do something about the rising threat of violence, and in 1934 the nation's lawmakers enacted the first law aiming to curtail the availability of weapons that seemed to suit only one purpose: killing people.

Controlling Guns

Over the years, the federal government has made relatively few laws restricting gun possession and use. The reason is the Second Amendment. Most often, the nation's highest courts have ruled that the country's founders, in writing the Constitution and the Second Amendment, intended for any gun laws to be made at the local level—by the state, not the federal government.

Nevertheless, at times Congress has decided that the national good required a federal gun-control law. These laws have often been inspired by a particularly shocking incident or by a particularly threatening wave of violence. Here are some of the measures that federal lawmakers have taken:

National Firearms Act, 1934. Congress passed this law and established the Bureau of Alcohol, Tobacco, and Firearms

(BATF) to enforce it. This law banned specific types of weapons favored by Prohibition-era gangsters, notably the machine gun, the sawed-off shotgun, and the silencer, a device that was screwed onto a gun barrel to muffle the sound of a shot. Lawmakers hoped to end violence among gangsters by banning their preferred weapons.

Federal Firearms Act, 1938. This law required that gun manufacturers and sellers be licensed by the government. This was viewed as a way for the government to have some control over how guns were bought and sold. In theory, it would help keep guns out of gangsters' arsenals, but in reality it was not nearly as effective as officials had hoped. The Federal Firearms Act also forbade felons to possess firearms or ship them across state lines, and the law made it a crime to possess stolen guns or ammunition. Oddly, the law did not prevent guns from being bought through the mail, a method of avoiding notice by the authorities.

Omnibus Crime Control and Safe Streets Act/Gun Control Act, 1968. In the 1960s, a rash of shocking political assassinations struck the nation: President John F. Kennedy in 1963, black separatist Malcolm X in 1965, civil rights leader Dr. Martin Luther King Jr. in 1968, and Senator Robert Kennedy in 1968. President Kennedy and Martin Luther King Jr. were shot by snipers with rifles; Malcolm X and Senator Kennedy were shot at close range by men with handguns who slipped through the two men's security teams. In addition, the civil rights movement of the time had led to violent racial clashes in many cities.

In an effort to prevent future violence of these kinds, Congress reinforced the 1938 gun-control law and added additional restrictions. These included the following: They prohibited gun dealers from selling handguns to persons under twenty-one and rifles to persons under eighteen; forbade felons, the mentally ill, and certain other categories of people from having guns; forbade the selling of guns to people who lived in another state; forbade mail-order gun sales, except between registered dealers; and required that dealers keep records detailing to whom they sold guns. They also forbade the import of military surplus weapons and cheap handguns—so-called Saturday night specials, thought to be a strong contributing factor to crime and impulsive shootings because of their low cost and easy availability.

Firearms Owners' Protection Act, 1986. This law, promoted by the National Rifle Association and other pro-gun groups, was one of the few federal laws to specifically make guns easier to buy and possess. Among other things, it allowed mail sales and sales to out-of-state buyers, and it reduced dealers' record keeping. It did, however, ban machine guns not owned before 1986.

Law Enforcement Officers' Protection Act, 1986. In the 1970s three men—a county coroner and two police officers—developed a new bullet that they thought would be a boon for the police. Coated with Teflon (the same stuff that keeps foods from sticking to frying pans), the bullets were intended to stop criminals in fleeing cars. Unfortunately, the bullets "worked too well," reports William Weir, author of *A Well-Regulated Militia.* "The Teflon-coated bronze bullets penetrated cars, penetrated the law-breakers in the cars, and penetrated the other side of the cars. They then bounced around off walls and sidewalks and put everyone in the vicinity in grave danger."[3] The bullets also penetrated the "bulletproof" Kevlar vests worn by the police. The "KTW" bullet (named after its three creators), also called the "cop-killer" bullet, received massive publicity, and Congress rushed a law through banning this and a number of other bullets that were thought to be a danger to the police.

Undetectable Firearms Act, 1988. Another new technology came to public attention in the late 1980s. A German company developed a new kind of hard plastic material that could be used for making guns. Previously, only metal was thought to be able to withstand the heat and force a gun emitted each time it was fired. With the new plastic, however, guns could be made lighter and thus more convenient. The first gun with this technology was the Glock 17, a nine-millimeter heavy-duty semiautomatic handgun (capable of firing several shots in quick succession). News reports indicated that the gun, because it was largely plastic, could travel undetected through airport security monitors. In fact, the Glock contained 19 ounces of steel as well as plastic and was readily detected. Nevertheless, the public and airline and law enforcement officials feared plane hijackings and other crimes that could be committed by an "undetectable" gun. Congress passed this law banning plastic guns that contain less than 3.7 ounces of detectable metal. It also banned guns that did not look like guns—"spy" guns made to look like cameras or pens, for example.

Gun-Free School Zone Act, 1990. Spurred by several incidents of gun violence occurring in and near schools, this law forbade firearms within one thousand feet of a school. The

The Brady Handgun Violence Protection Act was passed by Congress in 1993. The law requires handgun buyers to undergo background checks before obtaining a gun.

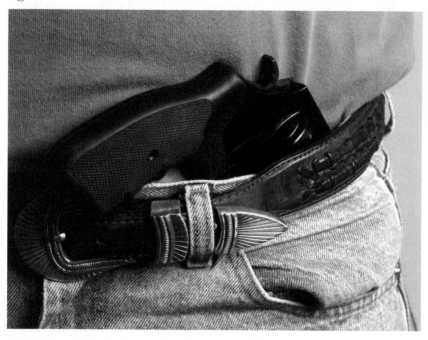

Supreme Court later ruled this law unconstitutional, saying that it interfered with the rights of individual states to regulate local matters. (The Court noted that forty states already had laws limiting weapon possession on or near school grounds.)

Brady Handgun Violence Protection Act, 1993. In 1981 a gunman trying to assassinate President Ronald Reagan seriously wounded Reagan's press secretary, James Brady. Brady survived the attack but was permanently paralyzed. By 1985 Brady's wife, Sarah, had joined Handgun Control, Inc., one of the most active pro-gun-control organizations. She soon became its best-known spokesperson and its president. James Brady, too, became an active participant in the organization. After more than ten years of lobbying Congress and battling with the National Rifle Association, the Bradys were proud to see the law passed at last, and with James Brady's name on it.

The law provides stricter regulation of handguns than ever before. Among other things, it requires a background check and a waiting period before a buyer can obtain a gun. The background checks are carried out electronically nationwide. Law enforcement authorities search for law infractions or other things that would make a customer ineligible to buy a gun.

Violent Crime Control and Law Enforcement Act, 1994. Originally, assault weapons were simply guns—rifles—developed for military use. But gradually, this type of gun became available to the general public. Whereas most hunting rifles, for example, are single-shot or double-shot guns (only one or two bullets are available to the gun at a time), assault rifles are semiautomatic, making several bullets—often up to one hundred or more—available to be shot in quick succession.

Following a 1989 incident in which a gunman with an assault rifle opened fire at a California school yard, killing five children and wounding twenty-nine others and a teacher, several states banned assault weapons. With this 1994 law, the federal government followed suit, banning semiautomatic rifles and handguns, with a few exceptions.

In addition to these federal laws, state and local governments have collectively passed more than twenty thousand gun-control measures. Some states specifically protect the right to own hunting weapons. Some require that all guns be carried in the open, but others require that guns be kept out of sight. Some make adults criminally liable if children get hold of household guns. Some states require special permits to own guns; others do not. A few places, such as Morton Grove, Illinois, have banned guns entirely. Some states have many very restrictive laws, but others have few and weak gun-control laws. The wide range of laws is testimony to the nation's lack of consensus about guns, violence, and personal rights.

The opposing sides of the gun-control debate today are most strongly represented by the National Rifle Association, which adamantly opposes gun control, and Handgun Control, Inc., which favors a handgun ban and other restrictive gun laws.

The NRA

Founded in 1871 by two Civil War veterans, the National Rifle Association (NRA) was established to encourage marksmanship for local "militia." For its first decades, the NRA was essentially a hobby organization. It sponsored shooting matches with local and international teams, and its members had a mutual interest in firearms and related activities such as hunting.

In the 1970s the National Rifle Association became seriously involved in political action, and today it is the strongest protector of gun owners' rights. The NRA is a lobbying organization—that is, it works to influence lawmakers to make laws that benefit its members. It is not the only gun owners' association, but it is by far the largest and most powerful. It has some 3 million members, from whom it receives dues and other contributions that give it a multimillion-dollar budget to use for protecting gun owners' rights at the governmental level. As Edward F. Leddy, author of *Magnum Force Lobby*, writes, "The existence of the National Rifle Association is the greatest single reason why the United States has not adopted the types of firearms restrictions which are common in many countries."[4]

The NRA is not alone in its efforts. Many groups lobby lawmakers in an effort to see their members' interests furthered. But some critics say that the NRA is too large and too powerful. Unquestionably, it has more money to spend on lobbying efforts than almost any other organization (the American Association of Retired Persons is one of the few that is bigger). And the NRA has a very active membership: Many NRA members are willing to inundate their senators and representatives with letters, telegrams, petitions, and phone calls, exerting pressure for the lawmakers to do what the NRA wants.

Many NRA members, however, do support some forms of gun control, and the NRA has also supported bills that mandate some controls. It supported a second Brady bill, for example, that established instant background checks instead of a several-day waiting period for gun purchasers. Yet at the same time, it exerted its powerful influence to water down a 1999 crime bill, which would have mandated stronger restrictions on gun sales at unregulated places such as gun shows and flea markets.

Handgun Control, Inc.

Today, the chief pro-gun-control organization is Handgun Control, Inc. (HCI). It has more than four hundred thousand members. Like the NRA, it is not the sole organization working to control fireams, but its concerted efforts have made it one of the largest, strongest, and best known.

HCI was established in 1974 as the National Council to Control Handguns. Its founder, Mark Borinsky, had been robbed at gunpoint and became determined to do something to end this kind of crime. The organization's initial goal was to ban handguns completely. It focused on handguns because they are the most common weapon used in crimes like robbery and murder, crimes of passion, and suicide. Long guns (rifles) are used more for hunting and competitive shooting and less in crimes; they also tend to be more expensive. Handguns can be expensive, too, but many are available for as little as fifty dollars.

The organization eventually faced "political reality,"[5] says sociologist Gregg Lee Carter. Although Americans will support some forms of gun restrictions, research has consistently shown that the majority do not support the kind of total gun ban that has been successful in some other countries. HCI modified its goal to the strict regulation of guns, and handguns in particular. It favored registration, background checks, age limits, and other restrictions that would keep guns only in the hands of "law-abiding citizens . . . for legitimate purposes."[6]

Over the next several years, the organization devoted itself to working with legislators to try to achieve various gun-control aims and to making itself better known as an organization. With each high-profile act of gun violence (John Lennon's murder in 1980 and the 1981 attempted assassination of President Reagan, for example), more people joined HCI and the gun-control movement. The organization gained its highest public recognition after Sarah Brady, wife of assassin victim James Brady, joined and became its president. Brady devoted herself to clamping down on the millions of unrestricted guns in American society. The Brady Act was the group's first major victory under Brady's leadership.

Like the NRA, HCI has its critics, and it is just as zealous in fighting for its goals. Josh Sugarman, executive director of the Violence Policy Center, an offshoot of HCI, even suggests that "the purpose for which the movement was created—saving lives—has been superceded by a new goal: beating the NRA."[7]

Will the efforts of laws and organizations like those described above solve the gun problem in the United States—if there is indeed a gun problem? Many people believe the difficulty lies not with guns but with basic problems in American society. At any rate, public awareness and education are often the first, vital steps to solving a problem. Only through a national dialogue will the nation reach a concensus about the place of guns in society.

1. Eric Westervelt, "Gun Control Series," *Morning Edition*, National Public Radio, June 17, 1999.

2. Quoted in Neal Bernards, *Gun Control*. San Diego: Lucent Books, 1991, p. 12.

3. William Weir, *A Well-Regulated Militia*. North Haven, CT: Archon Books, 1997, p. 103.

4. Quoted in Weir, *A Well-Regulated Militia*, p. 64.

5. Gregg Lee Carter, *The Gun Control Movement*. New York: Twayne, 1997, p. 75.

6. Quoted in Carter, *The Gun Control Movement*, p. 76.

7. Quoted in Carter, *The Gun Control Movement*, p. 103.

CHAPTER 1

How Does Gun Availability Affect Society?

"It is clear that guns kill alarmingly high numbers of Americans every year."

Gun Availability Contributes to Crime and Violence

Gun advocates are fond of the saying "Guns don't kill; people do." Yet tragic incident after tragic incident proves just the opposite. Consider these statistics from the Centers for Disease Control and Prevention and the National Center for Health Statistics:

- In 1995 the United States had 35,957 gun-related deaths, including suicides, murders, and unintentional deaths.
- In 1996, 10,744 people in the United States were murdered with guns, more than 7,000 of those with handguns.
- Every day fourteen American children and adolescents die in gun-related incidents.
- Firearm injury is the number-one cause of death for Hispanic and African American youth, ages fifteen to nineteen.
- Firearm injury is the number-two cause of death for Asian/Pacific and Caucasian youth.
- Violence is the leading cause of injury, death, and disability for all Americans.
- Some sources project that by the year 2003, firearm fatalities will be the leading cause of injury-related death unless the violence is curbed.

Guns Kill

Yes, in 1995 guns killed 35,957 people on American streets and in American homes, businesses, and schools. In comparison, 33,651 Americans were killed in the Korean War (1950–1953) and 58,148 in the Vietnam War (1954–1975). It is appalling to think that more people are killed in one year during peacetime in this country than were killed in a three-year war.

It is even more eye-opening to look at international gun-death statistics. The United States has the highest murder and gun-murder rates of any of the higher-income nations. In 1995 there were 13.7 firearm deaths for every 100,000 people. Men had a higher rate than women, and certain age and ethnic groups had the highest rates of all. Here is a further breakdown of American gun murders based on figures from the National Center for Health Statistics:

U.S. Firearm Deaths per 100,000 People	
Total	13.7
Females	3.9
Males	23.9
Whites	11.7
African Americans	29.1
African American males between the ages of 15 and 24	140.2

In contrast, for every 100,000 people in England, which has strict gun-control laws and few privately owned firearms, there were only .55 murders, only .07 of which were caused by guns, reports the *International Journal of Epidemiology*. That means that the U.S. gun-murder rate per person was almost thirty-five times higher than England's.

Gun Violence in the Home

It is clear that guns kill alarmingly high numbers of Americans every year, yet Americans continue to buy guns. In 1997 Americans owned about 240 million guns, and more than one-third of American households had at least one gun. Think

GUNS DON'T DIE...PEOPLE DO.

© Mike Ramirez. Reprinted by permission of Copley News Service.

about what that means. If you don't own a gun, it's likely that at least one of your neighbors does. And the numbers tell us how dangerous that is.

Research reported in the *New England Journal of Medicine* concludes that people with guns in their homes are five times more likely to experience a suicide and three times more likely to experience a homicide (murder) than people who do not own guns. Citing this data, the Coalition to Stop Gun Violence reports that "additionally, a gun kept in the home is 43 times more likely to kill a member of the household, or friend, than an intruder." Crime data indicate that the leading cause of firearm deaths is arguments, most often with family, friends, or neighbors. The coalition notes that "research indicates that the use of a firearm to resist violent assault actually increases the victim's risk of injury and death."[1]

Even highly trained police officers are often unable to protect themselves with their guns. The most common gun accident occurs when people are cleaning their guns. Average citizens, most of whom have received no gun training at all, are even less likely to be able to use a gun safely.

Guns Do Not Reduce Crime

Some people wrongly believe that allowing more people to have guns will reduce crime and violence. They often point to the example of Florida. Gun advocates say that Florida was a state brimming over with gun-related violence until the passage of a 1987 law allowing nearly anyone to carry a concealed weapon. After that law was passed, they say, Florida's violent crime rate decreased significantly. But that is not true.

Between 1987 and 1992, the violent crime rate, including murder, assault, rape, and robbery, increased almost 20 percent. Every year since then, Florida has had the highest rate of violent crime in the nation, according to the FBI's Uniform Crime Report. As Florida has acted to toughen its gun laws, the murder rate has gone down somewhat, but the state, which still has its lax "concealed-carry" law, is still the "murder capital" of the nation. The tragedy is that gun sellers exploit people's fears to try to influence them to buy a product that is much more likely to harm them or their children than it is to protect them.

1. Coalition to Stop Gun Violence, "The Facts." www.gunfree.org/csgv/basicinfo.htm.

"[Guns] can make it easier for people, particularly those who are relatively weak physically, to be able to defend themselves."

Gun Ownership Protects People from Crime and Violence

It was October 1991. Suzanna Gratia and her parents were at a restaurant in Killeen, Texas, planning to have lunch. Suddenly, gunfire erupted. By the time it ended, Gratia's parents and twenty-one other people were dead. Gratia owned a gun, but she had left it in her car. She believes to this day that if she had carried the gun into the restaurant, some, if not all, of the twenty-three victims would be alive.

Gratia's belief is not unfounded. Many studies point to the value of guns in stopping crime. One of the most thorough studies was conducted by Professor John R. Lott Jr. of the University of Chicago. He analyzed crime data for all 3,054 counties in the United States for the years 1977 through 1994. What he found convinced him that guns can play an important role in preventing and reducing crime and violence.

"One can argue that having guns makes it easier for bad things to happen sometimes," Lott says, "but on the other hand, guns can prevent bad things from happening. They can make it easier for people, particularly those who are relatively weak physically, to be able to defend themselves. . . . Allowing would-be victims to defend themselves with guns against criminals . . . has a deterrent effect."[1]

Criminologist Gary Kleck of Florida State University analyzed National Crime Survey data from 1979 to 1985. His research shows that people use guns to defend themselves against criminals as many as 2.5 million times a year. That's 6,850 times a day! This "use" may range from simply saying, "I have a gun," to showing the weapon, to actually shooting at the criminal. Kleck discovered that "for both robbery and assault, victims who used guns for protection were less likely to be either attacked or injured than victims who responded in any other way."[2] Lott's findings confirmed this. He reports, "98 percent of the time that people use guns defensively, they merely have to brandish a weapon to break off an attack."[3]

Some legislatures have even been bold enough to take advantage of the effect gun ownership has on deterring crime. In 1982 the city of Kennesaw, Georgia, a suburb of Atlanta, passed an unusual law requiring all heads of household to keep at least one gun in the house. According to Kleck, the residential burglary rate dropped 89 percent in Kennesaw.

Vulnerable Victims Benefit from Guns

Bonnie Elmasri was a battered wife. She applied for a gun permit to protect herself from her estranged husband, who had repeatedly threatened to kill her. In her state, a person had to apply to buy a gun and then wait forty-eight hours before picking up the gun. Before the forty-eight hours were up, Bonnie and her two sons had been murdered by the husband.

The best way for women to protect themselves from violent crime is to own—and be properly trained in the use of—a gun. Often, women are counseled to not resist an attacker, but research shows this to be bad advice. Lawrence Southwick, a professor at State University of New York, Buffalo, examined 1979–1987 data from the Justice Department's National Crime Victimization Study. Southwick "found that the probability of serious injury from an attack is 2.5 times greater for women offering no resistance than for women resisting with a gun."[4] Those who resisted *without* a gun, however, were four times more likely to be injured. (Southwick's analysis showed that men, too, fared better with a gun, but the difference was not as great.)

Criminals, like the rest of us, want to get things the least expensive way. They prefer to attack weak victims who won't "cost" them serious injury or death; if they know a person is armed with a gun, they are less likely to choose that person as their victim. In 1985 the National Institute for Justice reported that "three-fourths of felons polled agreed that 'a criminal is not going to mess around with a victim he knows is armed with a gun.'"[5]

In fact, between 1973 and 1992, the rate of gun ownership in the United States increased by 45 percent and the number of handguns increased by 110 percent (from 37 million to 78 million); as a result, the national homicide rate fell by 10 percent, according to research done by professors Daniel D. Polsby and Dennis Brennan. They also found that "areas with relatively high gun ownership rates tended to report relatively low violent crime rates."[6]

Guns in Florida

This is confirmed by studies of crime rates in Florida, a heavily armed state that used to be awash in violent crime. In 1987 the state passed a "concealed carry" law, which enabled ordi-

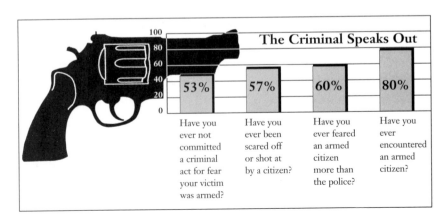

The Criminal Speaks Out

	Have you ever not committed a criminal act for fear your victim was armed?	Have you ever been scared off or shot at by a citizen?	Have you ever feared an armed citizen more than the police?	Have you ever encountered an armed citizen?
	53%	57%	60%	80%

nary citizens to easily get permits to carry concealed weapons for self-defense. (This is in contrast to most states' gun permits, which only allow guns to be kept at home or safely locked in a car trunk, for example. They do not allow citizens to carry a loaded gun in a handbag or briefcase.) Since 1987 Florida has granted concealed-carry permits to almost four hundred thousand people. The very idea of this makes some people nervous, but in Florida, it has worked. The murder rate has fallen 36 percent, according to FBI crime statistics. "Concealed carry laws are one way of making sure citizens can protect themselves from the real dangers,"[7] writes newspaper columnist Samuel Francis.

Lott's research also confirmed the benefits of concealed-carry laws. He explains,

> The only gun control law that I looked at that provides any real benefit was the passage of these right-to-carry laws. What I find is that those places that issued the most permits have the biggest drop in crime and that over time, as more permits are issued in states, there's a very strong relationship between issuing more permits and a further drop in violent crime.[8]

The same tendency appears to be true in many parts of the world. Lott points out that "Finland, Switzerland, and New Zealand have high long gun and handgun ownership rates and low violent crime rates. Israel has one of the highest long gun and handgun ownership rates in the world and has a murder rate that's 40 percent below Canada's."[9] (Canada has a very low gun ownership rate.)

Gun Dangers?

A masked, knife-wielding robber entered a Lancaster, Pennsylvania, grocery store and demanded money. The store owner's son pretended to reach for money, but instead he pulled out a handgun. He pointed it at the intruder, who said, "Hey, you can't shoot me!"[10] He tore off his mask, dropped his knife, and ran out of the store.

Gun-control advocates say that owning a gun is a dangerous thing. They say that people who own guns are more likely to be injured or killed by their own gun or to injure or kill someone else. But these ideas aren't true. Lott's research showed that

- just 17 percent of Chicago's murder victims from 1990 to 1995 were family members, friends, roommates, or neighbors;
- only one gun-permit owner nationwide has ever shot a police officer;
- no more than 4 percent of gun deaths can be blamed on the homeowner's gun;
- in 1995 just 200 children nationwide were killed in firearms accidents while 2,900 died in car accidents, 950 died from drowning, and more than 1,000 died in fires;

The fact is that a gun is more likely to protect the average careful, law-abiding person than it is to harm him or her. Francis points out, "Carrying a firearm doesn't mean you resolve all conflicts by blasting whoever you're conflicting with, but . . . some conflicts can't be resolved except by force, and every schoolboy discovers that truth early during recess, even if his mother never learns it."[11]

1. Quoted in Ruben Rosario, "Economist Analyzes Gun Laws, Sets Off Debate," *St. Paul Pioneer Press*, August 10, 1998, p. 4B.

2. Quoted in Samuel Francis, "Finding Safety in Gun Ownership," *Washington Times*, March 10, 1995, p. A21.

3. John R. Lott Jr., "Will More Guns Mean Less Crime?" *Consumer's Research*, December 1998, p. 18.

4. Lott, "Will More Guns Mean Less Crime?" p. 18.

5. Gun Owners Foundation, "Firearms Fact-Sheet," February 1997. www.gunowners.org/fstb.htm.

6. Daniel D. Polsby and Dennis Brennan, "Taking Aim at Gun Control," Heartland Institute Policy Study, no. 69, October 30, 1995, p. 8.

7. Francis, "Finding Safety in Gun Ownership," p. A21.

8. Quoted in Rosario, "Economist Analyzes Gun Laws, Sets Off Debate," p. 4B.

9. Quoted in *Human Events*, "Chicago Professor Discovers More Guns Means Less Crime," June 19, 1998, p. 6.

10. Quoted in *American Rifleman*, "The Armed Citizen," May 1999, p. 8.

11. Francis, "Finding Safety in Gun Ownership," p. A21.

"If young people did not have such easy access to guns, they would not take them to school and intimidate, injure, and kill teachers and students."

School Violence Is Caused by Gun Availability

Bethel, Alaska, February 19, 1997: A high-school student shoots and kills the school principal and a student in the school's commons area. *Paducah, Kentucky, December 1, 1997:* A fourteen-year-old boy opens fire on a before-school student prayer group, wounding five and killing two students. *Jonesboro, Arkansas, March 24, 1998:* Two boys, ages eleven and thirteen, shoot and kill four students and a teacher and wound ten other students. *Littleton, Colorado, April 20, 1999:* Worst of all, fourteen students and one teacher are shot and killed and another twenty students are wounded when two students open fire.

These are only four of the numerous high-profile school shootings that have occurred in recent years. And these bare statistics tell only part of the story. They don't tell anything about the thousands of students and families whose lives are changed forever, who spend years jumping at popping sounds, who never again feel safe in the place that, besides their home, they should feel safest.

All of these traumas occurred for one reason: The young shooters had access to guns.

Guns in Schools

According to FBI statistics, each year around six thousand gun-related incidents in the nation's schools come to the attention of law enforcement officials. There are uncounted numbers of other incidents that are not officially reported. No wonder many students tell pollsters that they "fear violent attacks traveling to and from school as well as within school itself."[1]

According to a 1997 survey by the Centers for Disease Control and Prevention, 8 percent of high-school students—that's 1 in 12—admitted carrying a gun to school in the month before the survey. The FBI reported that in 1995, 43,211 juveniles were arrested for weapons violations. That's a lot of students with a lot of guns—and it doesn't count the young people who carried guns but were not arrested.

Numbers like these prove that teenagers have easy access to guns. In fact, in many states it's legal for young people to own guns. In the states where hunting is a strong part of the people's heritage, children as young as eight, nine, and ten routinely handle guns and own their own hunting rifles. This is insanity. Children don't have sound enough judgment to be handling these lethal weapons. And when they become teenagers, the dangers become even greater.

Mature teens may exercise judgment as strong as that of any adult. But for most teens, the adolescent years are a roller coaster of emotional turmoil. Their bodies and lives change so dramatically during these years that they often have a hard time dealing with the changes. They are deeply depressed one moment, manically excited the next, and burning with anger a moment later—and they have little control over these emotions. They have energy to burn, and they often act out their emotions in physical ways: They dance wildly, weep or giggle for hours, throw themselves into athletic encounters—and fight. Psychiatrist Sabine Hack says, "One thing we know about adolescents is that when something bad happens, they often get tunnel vision and see it as the only thing. . . . They feel stuck and desperate, and they don't see any way out." She adds, "All adolescents want to be like other adolescents. . . . Seeing that someone else has done something, even something horrific like shooting people at school, may give kids the idea, and make them feel that this is their escape."[2] Toss a gun into this emotional mix and you often get murder or suicide.

Teens' anger and depression are not only worrisome, they are also dangerous. Teens and guns are simply a volatile combination. The Center to Prevent Handgun Violence reports that nearly three thousand teens use guns to commit suicide every year. In its 1991 report "Juvenile Offenders and Victims," the U.S. Department of Justice's Office of Juvenile Justice and Delinquency Prevention reports that 78 percent of murders committed by juveniles involved a gun.

Where Do They Get Them?

Where do teens and children get all these guns? Not surprisingly, most get them at home: "School security experts and law enforcement officials estimate that 80% of the firearms students bring to school come from home, while students estimated that 40% of their peers who bring guns to school buy them on the street,"[3] states one writer. The most highly publicized school shootings fit this pattern:

• Jonesboro, Arkansas, March 24, 1998. The two cousins stole guns from their grandfather's home.

• Littleton, Colorado, April 20, 1999. The two students purchased their guns illegally.

• Conyers, Georgia, May 20, 1999. A fifteen-year-old used guns taken from his stepfather's gun cabinet to shoot and wound six schoolmates.

Twenty, thirty, forty years ago, these types of incidents were all but unheard-of. Children and teens were just as emotional in those days as they are today. The difference is that today more than 240 million guns circulate in American society. A report in the *Journal of the American Medical Association* stated that "an estimated 1.2 million elementary-aged, latchkey children have access to guns in their homes."[4] Nearly anyone who wants to obtain a gun can, even a child who doesn't truly understand a gun's lethality or an emotionally unstable teen who is angry with his or her parents, classmates, and teachers.

End Easy Access

The fact is, if young people did not have such easy access to guns, they would not take them to school and intimidate, injure, and kill teachers and students. It is essential that society find a way to prevent guns from getting into young people's hands. Congress restricts gun dealers from selling handguns to persons under twenty-one, but in many states minors may still purchase guns at unregulated venues such as flea markets. Furthermore, although Congress has set limits on the gun-*buying* age, many states allow children to *own* guns

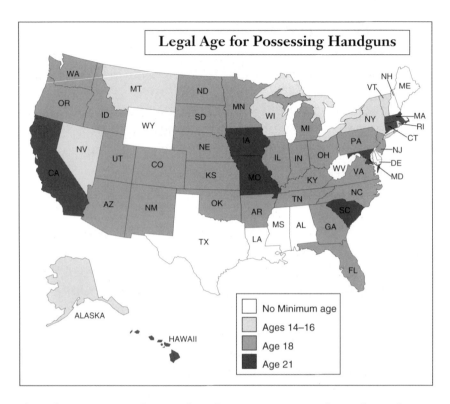

Legal Age for Possessing Handguns

Legend:
- No Minimum age
- Ages 14–16
- Age 18
- Age 21

they have received as gifts. Congress must close these loop-holes in the law.

Another effort is to require that adults who own guns store them in such a way that young people cannot get them. Kathy Kauffer Christoffel is the founder of the Handgun Epidemic Lowering Plan, a medical network in Chicago. She says, "We need to start recognizing that when a child gets a gun, an adult somewhere is responsible, maybe the parent or neighbor who didn't lock it up, or the unscrupulous person who sold it to them."[5] If the adult fails to safeguard his or her firearms or, worse yet, gives or sells a gun to a youngster, he or she should be prosecuted as a negligent criminal. This kind of law would have prevented the Jonesboro killings. If the two boys had not been able to get the grandfather's guns, they would not have killed.

The American people must support efforts like these and any others that will safeguard children from school violence.

Going beyond laws, the country must also look at schools and find ways to assure that no guns are on their premises. Some schools today have police guards or metal detectors that check students for weapons when they enter the school. Some critics say that precautions like these make schools feel more like prisons than joyful places of learning. But to save our children and make them know they are secure, perhaps that is a price worth paying.

Conclusion

America is a land of 240 million guns, any one of which could be used to cause another tragedy like that in Littleton, Colorado, or Paducah, Kentucky, or any of the other scenes of school violence. Americans must see to it that young people cannot get guns, and if they do, they cannot take them into our schools.

1. Coalition to Stop Gun Violence, "Guns in Schools." www.gunfree.org/csgv/bsc_sch.htm.

2. Quoted in Tamar Lewin, "Bloodshed in a Schoolyard," *New York Times*, March 26, 1998, p. A23.

3. Donna Harrington-Loeuker, "Blown Away," *American School Board Journal*, May 1992, p. 22.

4. Quoted in Coalition to Stop Gun Violence, "Guns in Schools."

5. Quoted in Lewin, "Bloodshed in a Schoolyard," p. A23.

"The availability-of-guns explanation assumes that other-wise harmless, even nearly normal, kids become dangerous only in the presence of guns. The truth is that these kids are dangerous anyway."

School Violence Is Not Caused by Gun Availability

In recent years, there has been an alarming number of school shootings. Many people blame these tragedies on young people's ability to obtain guns. But that couldn't be further from the truth. There's an old saying that's very true: Guns don't kill; people do. If the young people who shot their classmates and teachers hadn't had guns, they would have found another way to wreak their terrible violence. Only early, effective intervention in the lives of violent youth can prevent these tragedies.

School Shootings Are Extremely Rare

While not belittling the seriousness and tragedy of school violence, it is important to note that these incidents happen very rarely. An article in the *Los Angeles Times* points out, "Of 20 million middle-school and high-school students, fewer than a dozen have been killed at school this year [1998]. Of 20,000 secondary schools [high schools] nationwide, only ten have reported a murder on campus."[1] Almost half of the nation's schools reported no crime of any sort in the 1996–1997 school year. Of the incidents that do occur, only a small number involve guns. School violence, while serious, is not an epidemic threatening all children.

In 1998 the Centers for Disease Control and Prevention reported that "less than one percent of all homicides among school-aged children (five to nineteen years of age) occur in or around school grounds or on the way to and from schools."[2] *Newsweek* magazine reports that in 1996 "only 10 percent of schools registered even one serious violent crime; on average a high-school senior is 200 times as likely to be admitted to Harvard as to be killed in his school."[3] Only a very few, seriously disturbed students bring guns to school with the intent to harm others—and carry out that intent.

Referring to a tragic event in Jonesboro, Arkansas, where two boys shot fourteen students and a teacher, killing five of them, psychologist and novelist Jonathan Kellerman writes, "The *world* didn't fire 134 bullets at innocent children and teachers; two individuals did. And we'd better pay close attention to them and others like them in order to learn what created them and how to handle them." He continues, "The sad truth is that there *are* bad people."[4]

Cold-Blooded Killers

No one would deny that the acts committed by the young killers in Jonesboro in 1998, in Paducah, Kentucky, in 1997, and in Littleton, Colorado, in 1999 were bad acts. But most people shy away from the idea that the young shooters may have been bad people. Kellerman suggests that most of these school killers tend to be cold-blooded—what psychologists call psychopathic, sociopathic, or sufferers of antisocial personality disorder, the term currently in favor with mental health professionals. People identified in this way often have no real emotional ties to others, have patterns of cruel treatment of animals and people, lie without remorse, and get in trouble with authority—parents, school, and the law. These people know the difference between right and wrong, but they don't care. They are more concerned about wrongs they believe have been done against themselves. They often relish the power they feel they have over others because of their cruelty.

In most of the instances of school violence in which students have carefully planned and carried out mass shootings, the young people involved do exhibit these kinds of traits. As one example, Kellerman points out that Kip Kinkel appears to follow this pattern. Kinkel is the fourteen-year-old from Springfield, Oregon, who first murdered his parents and then went to school and shot up the cafeteria, killing two students. Kinkel had a pattern of abusing animals, he bullied his parents, he had no close school friends, and he was often in trouble with school authorities.

In his years of practice as a child psychologist, Kellerman encountered a number of young people he believed could very well turn out to be mass killers like Kinkel or the boys at Jonesboro if their behavior did not turn around. These cases were rare, he said, but they were truly frightening because these children had no feeling about hurting others. The fortunate thing is that there are almost always warnings. If people pay attention to these signs and act on them, school tragedies can be avoided.

Kids Who Want Guns Get Them

Helen Smith, another psychologist, agrees with Kellerman's assessment. She says that people who think keeping guns away from kids would solve the problem make two wrong assumptions: first, that young people have easier access to guns than they did in the past, and second, that if young people could not obtain guns, they wouldn't kill.

She points out that while there are more guns in the United States now than there were twenty or thirty years ago, "the percentage of households having guns is about the same as it was decades ago."[5] She also points to the time of the Vietnam War, when young people were not only holding peaceful demonstrations but were listening to antiwar activists like Jerry Rubin, who was calling for young people to "burn plastic suburbia down,"[6] and to Black Panthers who were fighting for black Americans' rights and were urging their followers to use any means to achieve their goals.

"For the availability-of-guns explanation to make sense," she writes,

> it [would be] necessary to believe that [during Rubin's time] . . . groups of depraved teens sat around plotting killing sprees like that in Littleton and then gave up in dismay and slunk off to college when they realized that they would be unable to come up with any guns. How likely is that? The fact is, despite Rubin's exhortations, teens weren't thinking that way back then. If they had been, they could have gotten guns.[7]

Regarding the second assumption, Smith says,

> this assumes that in the absence of easily available guns, would-be killer teens wouldn't have done anything. The Littleton killers disproved that by producing an arsenal of explosive devices. . . . The availability-of-guns explanation assumes that otherwise harmless, even nearly normal, kids become dangerous only in the presence of guns. The truth is that these kids are dangerous anyway.[8]

Indeed, Smith quotes one of the jailed school shooters she counseled. This boy told her, "So let them take away my guns. I would just use a knife."[9] Smith warns that the problem lies not with guns, but kids today "reach the breaking point without adults even noticing."[10]

No One Noticed

And that's one of the keys to the problem. Over and over, we discover too late that killer kids have given plenty of warning before committing their terrible deeds. Kip Kinkel wrote in school papers that he was going to kill everyone. Eric Harris had a website saying the same thing, and he and Dylan Klebold, the shooters in Littleton, Colorado, had made a movie for one of their classes in which they used real guns to pretend to kill the school's athletes. These kids told the people around them what they were going to do, but no one noticed.

Keeping guns out of kids' hands may make some people feel better and may even prevent a few acts of impulsive violence, but it won't solve the problem. Reducing teen access to guns is like putting a Band-Aid on a bear bite. Only by all of us working together—parents, schools, society as a whole—can we hope to end the threat of violence in our schools.

1. Carol Tavris, "Violence Is a Symptom, Not an Inevitability," *Los Angeles Times*, March 24, 1998.

2. Centers for Disease Control and Prevention, "Facts About Violence Among Youth and Violence in Schools," May 21, 1998.

3. Jerry Adler and Karen Springen, "How to Fight Back," *Newsweek*, May 3, 1999, p. 37.

4. Jonathan Kellerman, *Savage Spawn: Reflections on Violent Children*. New York: Ballantine, 1999, p. 33.

5. Helen Smith, "It's Not the Guns," Nando Media, May 1999. www.nandotimes.com.

6. Smith, "It's Not the Guns."

7. Smith, "It's Not the Guns."

8. Smith, "It's Not the Guns."

9. Smith, "It's Not the Guns."

10. Smith, "It's Not the Guns."

CHAPTER 2

Is Gun Control Constitutional?

"Americans should think long and hard before questioning the right to bear arms."

Gun Ownership Is Protected by the Second Amendment

Shortly after our ancestors wrote and voted to accept the Constitution that guides the U.S. legal framework, they added ten amendments, or changes. These amendments are called the Bill of Rights. The ten amendments lay out a group of important rights that the founders of the country wanted to be sure were guaranteed to all citizens. The second of these amendments relates to a person's right to own guns.

The amendment states, "A well regulated Militia, being necessary to the security of a free State, the right of the people to keep and bear Arms, shall not be infringed."

Assurance of Freedom

The country's founders had good reasons for putting this guarantee into writing. They had fought for independence from England because the British had denied the American colonists' individual rights. Among other things, the British had wanted to keep their soldiers in American homes, draft American men to fight in England's wars, and tax the colonists without letting them have a say in the government they were financing. If they had obeyed all of England's rules, the colonists felt, they would have been little more than England's slaves, working for England's profit instead of their own.

Most of the people who had immigrated to America wanted to have the freedom to lead their own lives, work hard for their future and the future of their children, and make their own rules in cooperation with their neighbors. They resented the English king who tried to keep them tied to England. They wanted to establish their own free nation. Eventually, they knew that the only way they could do this was to fight England's armed soldiers.

The colonists created their own militias, or informal armies, and won the war against England. After their victory, they wanted to ensure that no strong single power, like a king or a dictator, could ever gain power over the American people. They wanted to ensure that individuals in America would be free to live and work as they wished. They had to create a plan that would enable the people to stand up against any power that threatened their freedom. Their plan included guaranteeing that the people would always be able to have guns to protect themselves and their freedom if necessary.

America's founders, because of their experience with the British king, were suspicious of strong central governments and armies. They decided it would be best not to create a standing army (one that remains in effect even when there is no war). That created too much danger that a corrupt king or president could once again turn the people into slaves. Instead, they planned for the country to be defended by militias, local groups made up of armed citizens that would be prepared to fight at any time but would have no official status. They would be trained and led by local leaders, not by government officers.

A Long Tradition

In deciding this, the founders were following a long tradition. In the seventh century, for example, laws of the Anglo-Saxons (forbears of the English) required that all free men must own weapons and be prepared to use them in defense of their king. In a history of the English army, Francis Grose writes, "Every landowner was obliged to keep armor and weapons according to his rank and possessions. . . . They had their stated ties for performing their military exercise; and once a year, generally in spring, there was a general review of arms throughout each county."[1]

This tradition continued right up to the time of the American colonies. Historian Gregg Lee Carter writes,

> The restored Anglo-Saxon tradition of all free men having the right, and even the duty, to keep and bear arms was transferred to colonial America, where all the colonies individually passed militia laws that required universal gun ownership. Hunting was essential to many families, and in light of immediate threats from the French, Dutch, Spanish, and Native Americans, it is not surprising that colonial militia statutes required that all able-bodied men be armed and trained.[2]

It was only natural that the new nation keep this concept intact—that all the citizens should help protect the nation rather than rely on a professional army, which, the people feared, could very well become their enslavers.

The Supreme Court and the Second Amendment

The intent of the nation's founders when writing the Second Amendment is clear: to ensure the safety of the nation by allowing—even requiring—all able-bodied citizens to be armed and ready to fight when needed. Yet the Bill of Rights does not "give" Americans the right to bear arms any more than the Declaration of Independence "gives" Americans the right to life, liberty, and the pursuit of happiness. As the editors of *New American* magazine explain, "The Second Amendment does not *grant* a right to keep and bear arms, but rather *recognizes* that pre-existing right [emphasis added]."[3] In other words, an individual's right to own guns existed even before the Constitution was written, and the federal government has no place interfering with that right.

In keeping with the spirit of the Second Amendment, as well as the founders' distrust of a central government and emphasis on local government, the Supreme Court has consistently ruled that only the states and local governments may make rules regarding gun ownership; the federal government cannot. A number of people convicted of gun crimes in their home states have tried to get their cases reviewed by the Supreme Court. In most cases, the Court has refused to look at the cases, saying it has no jurisdiction in such matters. In the few cases that it has heard, the Court has most often ruled that the federal government has no authority in gun cases. In the few exceptions, the Court has tended to rule that the Second Amendment refers to "a well regulated militia," which, according to the founders' views, was not to be regulated by the federal government.

Healthy Mistrust of Government

Some may say that relying on history and old definitions is silly and out of date. These people say the United States is a strong country that has no need for a citizen militia. But as legal scholar Sanford Levinson points out, "It seems foolhardy to assume that the armed state will necessarily be benevolent. The American political tradition is, for good or ill, based in large measure on a healthy mistrust of the state."[4] He quotes Edward Abbey, a naturalist and political activist who coined the maxim, "If guns are outlawed, only the government will have guns."[5] Anyone who thinks Levinson is overly cautious should take another look at recent history:

• In 1936 General Francisco Franco took over the republic of Spain and turned it into a fascist dictatorship. He accomplished this by disarming the citizens.

• During World War II millions of European Jews were rounded up, taken to concentration camps, and tortured and murdered. A letter to the *Washington Times* asks, "Could the

Gun-control laws left millions of European Jews virtually defenseless against Hitler's Nazi regime during World War II.

Holocaust have occurred if Europe's Jews had owned thousands of then-modern military Mauser action-bolt rifles?"[6]

• In 1989 in Peking, China, thousands of prodemocracy students demonstrating in Tiananmen Square were fired on by soldiers. Hundreds were killed. If the Chinese people had been allowed to own guns, states attorney M. Wimershoff-Caplan, "their rulers would hardly have dared to massacre the demonstrators."[7]

The Right to Bear Arms and Public Safety

There are those who argue that, regardless of what the Constitution says, gun ownership should be restricted or even banned because guns contribute to violence in society. But Americans should think long and hard before questioning the right to bear arms. As Benjamin Franklin said, "Those who would sacrifice essential liberties for a little temporary safety deserve neither liberty nor safety." More recently, newspaper columnist D.J. Tice wrote something about another freedom that applies to the Second Amendment as well. These are words all Americans should heed: "Justice in America is in trouble when so few see that freedom can only be safe if we uphold the Constitution fearlessly and unfailingly, even when it produces unpopular and even frightening results."[8]

1. Quoted in Gregg Lee Carter, *The Gun Control Movement*. New York: Twayne, 1997, p. 28.

2. Carter, *The Gun Control Movement*, p. 30.

3. *New American*, "Antidote for Oppression," March 30, 1998, p. 31.

4. Sanford Levinson, "The Embarrassing Second Amendment," *Yale Law Journal*, vol. 99, p. 655.

5. Quoted in Levinson, "The Embarrassing Second Amendment," p. 648.

6. Quoted in Levinson, "The Embarrassing Second Amendment," p. 657.

7. Quoted in Levinson, "The Embarrassing Second Amendment," p. 657.

8. D.J. Tice, "Linehan Case Typifies Scary Impulse Courts Recently Indulging: Ignoring Law," *St. Paul Pioneer Press*, June 2, 1999.

"Legislative restrictions on the use of firearms do not trench upon any constitutionally protected liberties."

Gun Ownership Is Not Protected by the Second Amendment

"There is no reason why all pistols should not be barred to everyone except the police."[1] So wrote Supreme Court justice William O. Douglas in 1972. The Supreme Court is the highest court in the United States. Its cases deal with constitutionality—that is, it determines if laws are in agreement with the U.S. Constitution.

The Constitution, as the founding fathers wrote and approved it, did not deal with the issue of gun ownership. But shortly after the Constitution was accepted, the founders attached the Bill of Rights, a group of ten amendments, or changes, that laid out specific rights guaranteed to American citizens. These included freedom of speech, freedom from unreasonable search by the police, the right to refuse housing government soldiers, and a number of other items that the founders considered basic and essential rights. The second of these amendments states, "A well regulated Militia, being necessary to the security of a free State, the right of the people to keep and bear Arms, shall not be infringed."

In the past few decades, as violence in American society has soared, this amendment has come under close scrutiny. What does it mean? Is *every* American allowed to own arms? Are all types of firearms, from handguns to assault rifles, covered by the term *arms?* There is a vocal group of people in this country who say that the answer to both these questions is yes. However, the Supreme Court has consistently ruled that this is not the case.

"A Well Regulated Militia"

Two key issues in this debate are the meaning of the word *militia* and the question of whether it is constitutional to place any kinds of limits on gun ownership.

To someone reading the amendment in the context of today's vocabulary, the wording of the amendment seems pretty clear: the right to own guns belongs to the militia. Today's militia is the National Guard, citizens who train together to learn military skills so that they can help the country in time of need.

But when there is an issue of constitutionality, legal scholars go back to the origins of the Constitution and try to interpret it in the way the country's founders intended. *Militia* had a somewhat different meaning two centuries ago when the Constitution was written. At that time, the militia included all able-bodied men. They were expected to drill regularly together under the leadership of a local officer, and they were expected to bring their own guns to use in defense of the country if needed.

Some scholars argue that this concept of militia should be the guideline today as well: All able-bodied people should be considered potential defenders of the country, and therefore all citizens should be allowed to have guns.

But anyone with an ounce of sense can see how false this argument is. People do not keep guns in their homes today in the spirit of being part of a militia. If they have guns, it is for personal pleasure, for the illusion of protection, or for criminal purposes. Only the National Guard is our militia today, and only the National Guard is guaranteed the right to have guns.

The Supreme Court has upheld the idea of the Second Amendment protecting gun possession for militia rather than for individuals. For example, in the 1939 case of *U.S. v. Miller*, the Court was asked to rule on the constitutionality of the National Firearms Act, which had been enacted in 1934. A man named Jack Miller took a sawed-off shotgun across the state line. This was outlawed by the National Firearms Act. Miller argued that the Second Amendment protected his right to own that gun. But the Court ruled that since a sawed-off shotgun had no practical use for a militia, it was not protected. "Certainly it is not within judicial notice that this weapon is any part of the ordinary military equipment or that its use could contribute to the common defense,"[2] the Court wrote.

The significance of this ruling was twofold: First, it showed that the amendment was preserving the rights of a militia, not individuals. Second, by affirming the National Firearms Act, it affirmed the right of the federal government to make laws relating to gun ownership.

Legal Restrictions on Gun Ownership

Another case that affirmed the government's right to deny gun ownership in some circumstances was *Lewis v. U.S.* (1980). In that case, a convicted felon said that the Gun Control Act of 1968, which forbade felons from possessing firearms, was unconstitutional because it prevented him from owning a gun. The Court ruled against Lewis. It ruled that common sense suggests that the founders did not have felons in mind when they wrote the Second Amendment. The Court went even further, stating that "legislative restrictions on the use of firearms do not trench upon any constitutionally protected liberties."[3] This statement means that the government *does* have a right to restrict gun ownership, contrary to the contentions of the National Rifle Association and other pro-gun organizations.

The Supreme Court hears many cases that have been tried in lower courts. If one of the parties involved in the lawsuit is not satisfied with the outcome of the initial case, that party can appeal to the Supreme Court to overturn the ruling of the lower court. Here is a sampling of some gun-control cases that the Supreme Court has either upheld or refused to review. (Refusal to review usually means that the Court does not believe there is valid reason to consider the case.)

• *U.S. v. Warin* (1976). The Sixth Circuit Court of Appeals ruled that the defendant had many complaints relating to the Second Amendment, but that all were "based on the erroneous supposition that the Second Amendment is concerned with the rights of individuals rather than those of the states."[4] (The Supreme Court has ruled in other cases that the states have the right to make restrictions on gun ownership.)

• *LaGioia v. Morton Grove, Ill.* (1981). The village of Morton Grove became the first community in the nation to outlaw possession of handguns. A gun-store owner sued on Second Amendment grounds. The Seventh Circuit Court of Appeals ruled that "possession of handguns by individuals is not part of the right to keep and bear arms."[5]

• *Farmer v. Higgins* (1991). In 1986 Congress passed a law forbidding the manufacture of new machine guns. A gun manufacturer sued. The Eleventh Circuit Court of Appeals ruled that the law was not unconstitutional.

Dump the Second Amendment?

It is clear that the Supreme Court, the highest court in the land, believes that individuals do not have a fundamental right to own guns. In fact, gun-control experts say that no gun-control law brought before the Supreme Court or other federal courts has ever been overturned on Second Amendment grounds. And Supreme Court justice Lewis Powell, in a speech to the American Bar Association, said, "With respect to handguns, [in contrast to] sporting rifles and shotguns, it is not easy to understand why the Second Amendment, or the notation of liberty, should be viewed as creating a right to own and carry a weapon that contributes so directly to the shocking number of murders in our society."[6]

But let's say the Court interpreted the laws in favor of gun ownership. Does that mean the nation should stick with a constitutional amendment that was written more than two hundred years ago, when conditions in American society were very different than they are now? Newspaper columnist Denis Horgan says absolutely not: "Dump the outdated Second Amendment—the only amendment that kills."[7]

1. Quoted in Violence Policy Center, "Who Dies? A Look at Firearms Death and Injury in America—Revised Edition, Appendix Four: The Second Amendment—No Right to Keep and Bear Arms," February 1999. www.vpc.org/studies/whocont.htm.

2. Quoted in Sanford Levinson, "The Embarrassing Second Amendment," *Yale Law Journal*, vol. 99, p. 652.

3. Quoted in Kristin Rand, "No Right to Keep and Bear Arms." Washington, DC: Violence Policy Center, 1992.

4. Quoted in Violence Policy Center, "Who Dies? A Look at Firearms Death and Injury in America."

5. Quoted in Violence Policy Center, "Who Dies? A Look at Firearms Death and Injury in America."

6. Quoted in Levinson, "The Embarrassing Second Amendment," p. 653.

7. Denis Horgan, "Forget Haphazard, Halfhearted Gun 'Control' and Dump Second Amendment Outright," *St. Paul Pioneer Press*, May 21, 1999.

CHAPTER 3

What Measures Would Be Effective in Reducing Gun Violence?

"Congress should listen to the people and make the laws that will make the United States a happier, safer nation."

The Government Should Pass Stronger Gun-Control Laws

Each day in the United States, more than three thousand gun-related crimes take place. These include murder, robbery, rape, and other kinds of assault. The country needs to make better gun laws to protect everyone from crime, and these laws should be the same all over the country.

The way things are today, each state makes its own gun laws. In some states, for example, it is legal for just about anyone to buy a gun; in others, it is legal for almost no one to buy one. The result of this mishmash of laws is that people who live in stricter states can take advantage of the weaker laws in other states. For example, New York laws generally prevent people from buying guns except in special, tightly controlled circumstances. But in Virginia, a nearby state, gun laws are much looser. So a New Yorker who wants a gun can simply take a short trip to Virginia and buy one. This makes no sense at all.

Poll after poll shows that the American people want guns to be controlled. A 1998 poll conducted by the National Opinion Research Center found that 85 percent of the general public wants stricter gun-control laws. This included gun owners, three-fourths of whom agreed. "Clearly, . . . the American public understands the need to strengthen this nation's gun control policies," notes Stephen Teret, director of the Johns Hopkins Center for Gun Policy and Research. "People readily accept strong regulation of the manufacture, sale, and distribution of these dangerous consumer products."[1]

Even if common sense didn't demand it, when such a significant majority wants stronger laws, Congress should listen to the people and make the laws that will make the United States a happier, safer nation. Following are a few of the laws that large numbers of people say they want.

Background Checks

Before anyone is allowed to buy a gun, a check should be made to ensure that they have never been convicted of a crime, been hospitalized for a mental illness, or have any other dangerous history. The Brady Act, which went into effect in 1994, mandated gun checks for gun purchases at gun stores. However, many loopholes exist. People who buy guns at gun stores *do* go through a background check, but people can buy guns at places besides gun stores. Those who buy a gun at a gun show or a flea market or from an acquaintance, those who buy a gun through a mail-order catalog or the Internet, and those who are given guns by relatives are not checked. This means that millions of guns are put into the hands of people whose backgrounds have not been checked. This is a dangerous situation for all of us.

Waiting Periods

Some states have waiting periods between the time a person applies to buy a gun and the time they actually get it. This is generally between three days and two weeks. In part, this waiting period was established to give law enforcement officials more time to do background checks. But in part, the waiting period, rightly called "a cooling off" period, was designed so that someone who is angry can't impulsively buy a gun and then turn around and shoot the object of his or her anger. By the end of a few days, the immediate passion of the anger is usually lessened. If the person acts on his or her anger, it is probably with words or fists—still not a happy thing, but much less dangerous than if they had a gun available.

Registration

Every gun should be registered to the person who owns it. Many states have laws requiring this, but some do not. If all guns were registered, they would be less likely to be used in crimes, or if they were, the police could more easily find the owners. Even if the gun was stolen from the owner, at least the police would have a starting point for their investigation. As President Bill Clinton remarked, "Tracing crime guns to their source and putting gun traffickers out of business for good will make our streets even safer."[2]

During the past seven years, the number of gun crimes has been decreasing slightly. Criminologists credit this trend in part to stronger efforts to trace guns. If registration laws were countrywide and were enforced for sales at gun shows and on the Internet as well as through gun stores, this trend would be reinforced and would drive our crime rate down even further.

Ban Certain Guns

Certain kinds of guns are involved in more crimes than others. These include

• "junk guns"—cheap handguns also called Saturday night specials. They acquired this name because they are so cheap that they are easily available to those who go on a drinking binge on Saturday night and act impulsively, foolishly, and often violently because of the drinking.

• "assault guns"—mililtary-style automatic weapons that can fire many bullets in a quick burst; these include machine-gun styles and automatic pistols such as TEC 9s and the Glock 9s used by many police departments. There is no good reason for most people to own guns like these. They are not used for any legitimate purpose, such as hunting or target shooting. They are simply intended to kill people.

As with the other inconsistent gun laws, different states have different policies toward these types of guns. They are banned in some states and easy to get in others. The country would be a lot safer if they were banned nationwide.

Ban Dangerous Accessories

Large-capacity ammunition clips are containers with any-where from a half-dozen to a hundred or more bullets that can be fed into automatic weapons at a high speed. They serve no useful purpose for sport or self-protection. Certain types of bullets, such as those that pierce bulletproof vests and shields that police officers use and those with soft tips that "explode" inside their target causing massive damage, also have no legit-imate purpose for the average citizen. Only criminals who want to kill the police have a need for such items. Therefore, they should be outlawed.

Require Safety Devices

Every gun should be required to have a safety device such as a trigger lock to prevent accidents. As Stephen Teret says, "We make aspirin bottles that cannot be operated by young chil-dren. Why can't we do the same with guns?"[3]

Many guns sold today do come with trigger locks or barrel guards (a plastic-encased cable that runs through the barrel of a handgun, preventing it from firing; it has to be unlocked to be removed). But the millions of guns that were sold before these safety devices became available are unsafe. Gun owners should be required to obtain such devices and use them with their present guns.

With the advance of technology, ever more sophisticated safety devices are becoming available. Already, some new handguns come with a microchip embedded in the handle that allows only the gun owner to fire it. Very soon, it will be the owner's voice command or other very specific personal "code" that "unlocks" the gun. If the law required this type of device to be put on all guns, not only would accidental shootings end, but stolen guns would not work for the thieves, so a lot of gun crime would disappear as well.

Raise Gun Ownership Age

In some states it is legal for a person to own a gun at age sixteen; in others he or she has to be twenty-one. In many states, especially those with a hunting culture, young children often own their own guns, usually gifts from their parents or grandparents. But even children who are well trained in how to handle a gun are still children, and children are immature. They do not have the judgment to know how to handle emergency situations. They are more impulsive than adults and are less likely to be as careful. They must go through the emotional seesaw of adolescence, which allows their emotions to rule over their reason in many instances. As Bob Walker, president of Handgun Control, Inc., notes, "We have to start looking at what can be done to reduce the access [of guns by youth]."[4] Children should not have guns.

Not every twenty-one-year-old is mature, but chances are that he or she has a better ability to exercise sound judgment than a child or even an older teenager. Federal law should mandate that no one under age twenty-one can own a gun.

Increase Penalties for Gun Crimes

Finally, our laws should be written so that the punishment for any crime in which a gun is used is double the punishment for that crime without a gun. If someone starts a bar fight and gets thrown in jail for ninety days, that punishment should be doubled to six months if he or she is carrying a gun at the time, and the penalty should be increased more if the gun is used to harm or kill someone.

After Minnesota enacted a new law imposing heavier penalties on crimes involving guns, state senator Randy Kelly noted, "What we're told [by the American people] is that we ought to be focusing time and attention on criminals with guns. . . . If you get some of these actors off of the street, you'll lower crime."[5] Minnesota did it, as have some other states. If the federal government were to make this policy standard for the whole country, the United States would see a major drop in crime from repeat offenders—those who go to prison, serve their short sentence, get out, and commit more crimes. This kind of extra penalty should also discourage a lot of first-time criminals from carrying guns.

If legislators would do what the people have shown they want and enact laws like those described above, this country would soon see a massive decrease in gun-related crime and violence.

1. Quoted in Join Together Online, "Gun Owners and General Public Want Stronger Gun Laws." www.jointogether.org.

2. Quoted in Associated Press, "Clinton Wants More Money to Trace Guns to Their Source," *St. Paul Pioneer Press*, February 22, 1999.

3. Quoted in Richard Morin, "Aiming for Tighter Control of Guns," *Washington Post National Weekly Edition*, March 31, 1997, p. 35.

4. Quoted in Ruben Rosario, "In Gun Debate, Sorting Out Views a Challenge," *St. Paul Pioneer Press*, August 3, 1998, p. 4B.

5. Quoted in Lucy Quinlivan, "Tougher Gun Laws Go into Effect," *St. Paul Pioneer Press*, January 2, 1999, p. 1A.

*"The truth is that this country has plenty of gun laws—
more than twenty thousand of them, in fact—but neither
the police nor the courts are enforcing them."*

Existing Gun-Control Laws Should Be More Strongly Enforced

There are people who say that if the United States only increased or improved its gun laws, it would be able to reduce crime. The truth is that this country has plenty of gun laws—more than twenty thousand of them, in fact—but neither the police nor the courts are enforcing them. Making more laws will not change that. If the present laws were enforced, no one would have to worry about gun crime, and the nation would not need any more laws.

Lack of Enforcement

In May 1999 Republican members of the House Judiciary Subcommittee on Crime reported that "[during the past year] there have been only a handful of prosecutions of the more than 250,000 felons and others who were detected illegally trying to buy a handgun and of the more than 6,000 juveniles who were expelled from school for carrying a firearm."[1] The committee concluded that law enforcement agencies had been lax in prosecuting violations of gun-control laws. Representative Bill McCollum (R-Fla.) agreed. He said that "doubling the size of the federal criminal code will not matter if the . . . administration refuses to vigorously enforce these laws."[2]

Many examples of lax enforcement can be cited. The *New York Times* reported one frightening example: In Chicago, "which has one of the nation's most restrictive gun laws," the *Times* said, "undercover officers recently went to suburban dealers and were able to buy guns while posing as members of city street gangs."[3] Only gun dealers who have no fear of being arrested would commit such blatant offenses.

Representative McCollum also pointed out that if people are rejected at a gun store, "these guys can go out and get a gun on the street, and that's what bothers me."[4] People buy and sell guns on the street in every city in the nation and even in small towns, and rarely do they have to worry about the police. People can even buy guns at a local flea market or garage sale. In some of these cases, the seller may be innocent of any purposeful wrongdoing, but the buyer can just as easily be a criminal as not. Worse, there are plenty of people who know exactly what they are doing: They drive to a state with weak or no gun laws, and they buy carloads of weapons that they take back home and sell to people they know are criminals. Their customers will use these guns for criminal and violent acts.

Even worse, the police rarely arrest these types of gun runners. The police get little support from the district attorneys and the courts. Many consider gun selling a small-potatoes crime. Some think it's hardly worth police and court time to prosecute these crimes. The penalty may be only a fine or a few months in jail—*if* the cases are won. National Rifle Association executive director Wayne R. LaPierre Jr. asserts, "They consider these nuisance cases. . . . That's shameful."[5]

Effect of Prosecution

All the evidence suggests that stronger enforcement of laws relating to guns would reduce crime dramatically. Several cities have experimented with programs aimed at eliminating illegal guns and ending gun crimes. They have had amazing results.

In the 1980s Boston had a serious problem with gang violence. In 1990 the city had the highest number of murders ever. Determined to turn the problem around, the city began the Youth Violence Strike Force. This plan had several components:

• Operation Night Light sent police and probation officers on nightly visits to the homes of young offenders to ensure that they were following the requirements of their probation.

• Operation Cease Fire set up meetings between police and gang members to spread the word that the police would go after them for any law infraction, including graffiti, truancy, and violation of noise laws, as well as gang violence.

• The Boston Gun Project involved the Boston police, Suffolk County district attorney's office, and federal agencies (the Bureau of Alcohol, Tobacco, and Firearms; the Drug Enforcement Administration; and the U.S. district attorney's office). Together, these law enforcement officials traced gun serial numbers and cracked down on the illegal gun market. They prosecuted gun crimes and exacted severe punishment.

• The Summer of Opportunity partnered local businesses in activities with at-risk youth.

Boston's Youth Violence Strike Force combined prevention, intervention, and enforcement. The U.S. Department of Justice reports that this three-pronged strategy has been effective: "Youth homicides have dropped some 80 percent citywide from 1990 to 1995, and in 1996, not a single youth died in a firearm homicide in the city. Violent crime in public schools decreased more than 20 percent in the 1995–1996 school year."[6]

The Justice Department reports success with similar programs in Jacksonville, Florida, and Salinas, California. Other programs have been used successfully in other cities. All of them emphasize strong enforcement of the laws.

Project Exile

Richmond, Virginia, has been plagued by growing gun violence for the past several years. The problem has been so bad that Richmond has been listed as one of the five worst cities in the country for per capita murder rates.

In 1997, the U.S. attorney's office in Richmond developed Project Exile. As with Boston's Youth Violence Strike Force, Project Exile involved city, state, and federal law enforcement officials. In fact, the Richmond plan placed its emphasis on getting gun crimes prosecuted in federal courts rather than local ones because federal penalties are stiffer. Assistant U.S. attorney David Schiller, who developed the program, writes,

> All felons with guns, gun/drug cases, and gun/domestic violence cases in Richmond are federally prosecuted. The project has fully integrated and coordinated local police, state police, federal investigators (BATF/FBI), and local and federal prosecutors to promptly arrest, incarcerate, detain without bond, prosecute, and sentence the armed criminal. An expedited reporting system . . . has decreased processing time from . . . several months to only several days. In court, bond is routinely and successfully opposed, and they obtain mandatory minimum sentences. The project has quickly, efficiently, and successfullly prosecuted a large number of gun crimes, with significant impact on criminal behavior.[7]

Richmond authorities say that Project Exile helped cut their gun murder rate by 36 percent in its first year, "one of the steepest declines in any city,"[8] according to the *New York Times*. Richmond police appreciate the emphasis that's being placed on prosecution and conviction of gun crimes, something the police typically have not been able to count on. The emphasis of the program, reports the *Washington Post*, is to "get the guns out of the hands of those who are carrying them illegally, people who are most likely to use the weapons in other crimes."[9] Felons found carrying guns automatically receive a five-year prison sentence in Richmond.

Wayne R. LaPierre Jr. says that Project Exile

> ought to be in every major city in the country where
> there's a major crime problem. The dirty little secret
> is that [in most cities] there is not enforcement of
> federal gun laws. What Exile's doing—which I think
> is great—is for the first time in a major American
> city, if a criminal picks up a gun, he'll do major time.
> It's a message the NRA [National Rifle Association]
> cheers, a message the police cheers. That's the magic
> of what they're doing in Richmond. The word is out
> on the streets of Richmond that the U.S. attorney is
> dead serious about stopping gun violence.[10]

Side Benefits

A positive side effect of plans like those described above is the
willingness of more people to participate in ending crime.
The emphasis on arrest, prosecution, successful convictions,
and long sentences makes witnesses more willing to testify in
court, bolstering the case against the criminal. *New York Times*
reporter Michael Janofsky writes,

> The program has also helped the authorities solve
> older cases. Once [a criminal named] Smith was sen-
> tenced, for example, witnesses no longer afraid of
> him [because they were assured of strong prosecu-
> tion, not a dismissal or a slap on the wrist] came for-
> ward with enough information to charge him with
> six murders, including two that could bring the
> death penalty.[11]

The success of programs like these depends on determined
enforcement of all gun laws. This can be achieved by a community that is willing to work together to do it. To make them
succeed, the police have to know that the courts and the district attorney's offices are willing to be tough in prosecuting
gun crimes, and the citizens and criminals have to know that

the police are going to make the arrests. Working together, it can be done. The United States can be safe again.

1. Quoted in Edward Walsh, "GOP Faults Enforcement of Gun Laws," *Washington Post*, May 28, 1999, p. A12.

2. Quoted in Walsh, "GOP Faults Enforcement of Gun Laws," p. A12.

3. Fox Butterfield, "New Data Point Blame at Gun Makers," *New York Times*, November 28, 1998, p. A9.

4. Quoted in Walsh, "GOP Faults Enforcement of Gun Laws," p. A12.

5. Quoted in Michael Janofsky, "Fighting Crime by Making Federal Case About Guns," *New York Times*, February 10, 1999, p. A12.

6. U.S. Department of Justice, "The President's Anti-Gang and Youth Violence Strategy: Success Stories," 1997. www.usdoj.gov/ag/success.htm.

7. David Schiller, "Project Exile," 1998. www.vahv.org/Exile.

8. Janofsky, "Fighting Crime by Making Federal Case About Guns," p. A12.

9. R.H. Melton, "Richmond Gun Project Praised," *Washington Post*, June 18, 1998.

10. Quoted in Janofsky, "Fighting Crime by Making Federal Case About Guns," p. A12.

11. Janofsky, "Fighting Crime by Making Federal Case About Guns," p. A12.

"It's time to send the bill for gun deaths and gun injuries to the gun makers."

Gun Manufacturers Should Be Held Responsible for Gun Violence

Guns kill more than two thousand people every year in the United States. The vast majority of these deaths would not occur if gun manufacturers didn't produce and sell 1.5 million guns each year.

The U.S. economic system is a materialistic one. Americans value material goods—the more the better. We can see this by looking at the extremely high percentage of Americans who own not one but two or more automobiles, two or more homes, two or more computers, and several television sets, video game systems, VCRs, cameras, and other gadgets. Americans have been taught to want the newest, the best, and the most of everything. Manufacturers make more and more products, Madison Avenue hypes them, and people buy them. Guns are no exception.

But the difference between too many guns and too many TV sets, and the difference between the newest cell phone and the newest high-tech handgun, is robbery, assault—and death. Just as cigarette companies are beginning to be punished for their decades of selling products that give people fatal illnesses, it's time to punish the gun manufacturers who are causing the deaths of thousands of Americans annually. The best way is through the courts.

Selling Guns to Criminals

Elisa Barnes, a New York attorney, brought a lawsuit against twenty-five gun manufacturers on behalf of her clients, relatives of gun-crime victims. Barnes sued the group of manufacturers because the specific guns used in the crimes weren't found. However, past courtroom experience taught Barnes that "under rare circumstances—such as when consumers can't identify the makers of an allegedly harmful product . . . manufacturers can be held liable according to their share of the market, rather than particularized proof of fault."[1] In other words, her suit would assign blame to each manufacturer depending on how big a part of the gun market it controlled.

Barnes accused "the entire industry of creating widespread risk with negligent marketing."[2] As newspaper writer Tom Hayes put it, "Handgun makers oversupply gun-friendly markets, mainly in the South, aware that the excess guns flow into criminal hands via illegal markets in New York and other states with stricter anti-gun laws."[3]

In fact, not only are gun makers *aware* that many of their products end up in criminal hands, some manufacturers seem to blatantly direct their advertising at criminals. One notorious example is an ad from Navegar, maker of the TEC 9, a "stylish" automatic weapon favored by criminals and mass murderers. The ad boasts, "Excellent resistance to fingerprints" and as "tough as your toughest customer."[4] Who, besides criminals, is concerned about fingerprint resistance?

Barnes found a former gun industry executive to help her case. He is Robert Hass, for eleven years a vice president of marketing for Smith & Wesson, one of the nation's biggest gun manufacturers. Hass asserted in court that the gun industry "is aware that the black market in firearms is not simply

Gun manufacturers exercise little control over the dealers and distributors to whom they sell.

the result of stolen guns but is due to the seepage of guns into the illicit market from multiple thousands of unsupervised federal firearms licensees"[5] who buy guns and sell them privately to shady characters.

Hass said that the gun industry could control this kind of dangerous dealing if it wanted to. With relative ease, it could keep records of all guns sold. Then it could cut off dealers who don't keep records of whom they sell the weapons to or who sell them to lawbreakers. Gun manufacturers already "discipline" dealers who sell their products at prices that are too low; they could also discipline them for not keeping appropriate records or for careless or criminal selling.

Economists working for Elisa Barnes testified that the sales in the states with weak gun-control laws "are higher than can be explained by legitimate demand—suggesting that a substantial proportion of sales in such states are not for legitimate purposes but for resale to the criminal market."[6] The economists testified that a review of the gun makers' own depositions "suggests that many if not all the manufacturers deliberately chose not to exercise any supervision over the distributors and dealers to which they sell."[7] The jury found that fifteen of the twenty-five gun makers named in the suit "distribute their product negligently,"[8] and the court ordered that five hundred thousand dollars be paid to two of Barnes's clients.

Public Nuisance

Barnes's case is one of the first against the gun industry. But many other cities and individuals are trying the same tactic to get rid of the gun menace. Chicago is one such city. Newspaper columnist Neal R. Pierce writes, "Chicago has strict laws against private handgun ownership. But gun makers, it's charged, are saturating surrounding suburban areas with more weapons than legal buyers could possibly want, knowing full well that thousands will be purchased by Chicago criminals who will use the weapons to kill, maim, or terrorize."[9]

Chicago is suing on the basis that the gun manufacturers are creating a public nuisance. Chicago's suit states that between 1994 and 1998, the cost was "at least $358 million to the city, [and] $75 million to Cook County, for added policing and court costs, ambulances, and hospital treatment of firearms wounds."[10] Chicago is trying to get the gun makers to take responsibility for the damage they have done by irresponsibly selling their guns.

Some critics say that cities like Chicago, Atlanta, New Orleans, and the others that are bringing lawsuits against gun makers are just trying to get easy money. But a spokesman for Chicago mayor Richard M. Daley said, "Chicago would not take a penny if we could just get the handguns off the streets."[11]

Irresponsible Manufacture

New Orleans is using a product liability argument: It is arguing that gun makers are violating a Louisiana law that "holds makers responsible for harm done by products unreasonably dangerous in design."[12]

This relates to the gun industry's "knowing refusal to equip their weapons with 'smart gun' technology such as personalized gun locks that prevent firing unless a ring fitted with a microchip is sensed, or the owner's fingerprints have been identified." Pierce writes, "The industry has long known about the safety devices but choose instead to use technology in a perverse way—to make guns ever more lethal."[13]

Other cities, too, are filing lawsuits against gun makers. Among them are Miami, St. Louis, Los Angeles, Baltimore, Minneapolis, San Francisco, and Bridgeport, Connecticut. A University of Chicago Law School expert told the *Chicago Tribune*, "The costs of the suits may 'bleed the industry to death' because gun makers' pockets aren't nearly as deep as those of tobacco companies."[14] No one likes to see companies fail, but in the case of the gun industry, that wouldn't be all bad. These companies are endangering people's lives in their efforts to gain profit.

The Gun Industry Makes a Profit by Promoting Violence

Tom Diaz is the author of *Making a Killing: The Business of Guns in America*. In a newspaper opinion piece, he aptly writes, "Like rampaging gamblers betting with other people's lives, the tycoons of the $1.4 billion gun industry have flooded America with more and more deadly guns for decades. . . . The industry has deliberately designed, manufactured, and marketed guns that are more lethal—more efficient at killing—to boost sagging sales."[15]

The industry has done this not only through excessive manufacturing and sales. It has also increased ammunition capacity of many guns, increased bullet size and firepower, and made more easily concealed, high-powered guns. "The firearms the industry sells today are very different from the mix of sporting, hunting, and target-shooting guns it sold scarcely twenty-five years ago," Diaz writes. "Today's mix emphasizes what NRA official Gary Anderson called 'the Rambo factor' at a 1993 industry shooting range conference. [Anderson pointed out:] 'If you look at the key words in arms and ammunition advertising, they are not *skill*, *accuracy*, or *marksmanship*. They are *power, speed,* and *firepower*.'"[16] These words are selected to appeal to the romanticism in the souls of many gun buyers who like to think that by purchasing a particular weapon, they can be invincible, like Rambo, the Sylvester Stallone movie character who single-handedly slays dozens of enemies.

Diaz concludes, "We're sick and tired of paying the costs of a decreasing minority's increasingly lethal toys—tired of paying for trauma centers, special policing, gun prosecutions, and communities devastated by gun violence."[17] As Miami-Dade mayor Alex Penelas told the *Wall Street Journal,* "It's time to send the bill for gun deaths and gun injuries to the gun makers."[18]

1. Paul M. Barrett, "Aiming High: A Lawyer Goes After Gun Manufacturers; Has She Got a Shot?" *Wall Street Journal,* September 17, 1998, p. A6.

2. Tom Hays, "Fifteen of Twenty-Five Gun Makers Found Liable in N.Y. Shootings," *St. Paul Pioneer Press,* January 5, 1999.

3. Hays, "Fifteen of Twenty-Five Gun Makers Found Liable in N.Y. Shootings."

4. Quoted in Barry Meier, "Guns Don't Kill; Gun Makers Do," *New York Times,* April 16, 1995, p. 3, sec. 4.

5. Quoted in Barrett, "Aiming High," p. A6.

6. Quoted in Barrett," Aiming High," p. A6.

7. Fox Butterfield, "New Data Point Blame at Gun Makers," *New York Times,* November 28, 1998, p. A9.

8. Hays, "Fifteen of Twenty-Five Gun Makers Found Liable in N.Y. Shootings."

9. Neal R. Pierce, "Wall of Shame," *St. Paul Pioneer Press,* November 24, 1998, p. 10A.

10. Pierce, "Wall of Shame," p. 10A.

11. Quoted in James Pilcher, "NRA Aims to Head Off Anti-Firearm Litigation," *St. Paul Pioneer Press,* February 5, 1999.

12. Pierce, "Wall of Shame," p. 10A.

13. Pierce, "Wall of Shame," p. 10A.

14. Quoted in Pierce, "Wall of Shame," p. 10A.

15. Tom Diaz, "Target: Guns: Opinion," *St. Paul Pioneer Press,* February 18, 1999, p. 8A.

16. Diaz, "Target," p. 8A.

17. Diaz, "Target," p. 8A.

18. Quoted in *American Rifleman,* "Hired Guns Aim for Your Guns," May 1999, p. 44.

"Gun manufacturers are simply making a product that people want to buy. Yet gun-control advocates want to punish them for it."

Gun Manufacturers Should Not Be Held Responsible for Gun Violence

"City officials want to gut-shoot gun manufacturers by suing them into bankruptcy,"[1] editorialized the Spokane, Washington, *Spokesman-Review*. Colorful language aside, there can be no question that the motives of those who are bringing lawsuits against gun manufacturers are less than noble. Putting gun manufacturers out of business is the aim of many of the lawsuits proliferating against the gun industry. The other motive is money. Those bringing their spurious claims hope to acquire some of the ridiculously large sums of money courts tend to award in cases like these. The suits are being brought by individuals victimized in gun-related crimes and by cities, including Chicago, Philadelphia, Atlanta, and New Orleans.

These cases have been inspired by successful lawsuits against the tobacco industry, in which the courts ordered tobacco companies to pay billions of dollars to the plaintiffs for having marketed an unsafe product. Both the tobacco and the gun lawsuits are frivolous and undemocratic and should never see the inside of a courtroom.

A Scurrilous Tactic

The gun industry is doing nothing wrong. The gun industry has not broken any laws—that is why it is facing civil lawsuits and not criminal prosecution. The American economic system is based on the concept of supply and demand. Gun manufacturers are simply making a product that people want to buy. Yet gun-control advocates want to punish them for it.

The *New York Times* reports that Atlanta was "the first of several cities to file lawsuits against the gun industry, seeking millions of dollars to reimburse local treasuries for the cost of the police and hospital services required because of gun violence."[2] But this scurrilous tactic is not going to work.

National Rifle Association executive vice president Wayne R. LaPierre Jr. states,

> What the mayors are going to find out is that a direct attack on the freedom to bear arms is the toughest briar patch they can jump into. They think that there is no cost, and this is a way to a quick buck, like tobacco money. But their cost, politically and economically, is going to be high, because we're determined to expose this for the sham that it is.[3]

Gun Manufacturers Are Not Responsible for How Their Products Are Used

In the past, a few suits have been lodged against gun manufacturers by individuals claiming a specific faulty gun caused a death or injury. This is understandable. The same type of suit has been brought against car manufacturers and hundreds of other products. If incompetent or negligent manufacturing leads to a gun that blows up in its owner's face, the manufacturer *should* be held liable. But if death or injury occurs because the person using the gun has been careless or is a criminal, it is simply not the gun maker's fault. As a letter writer told the *St. Paul Pioneer Press*, "We are treading on dangerous ground when we start blaming industries for the misuse of their product."[4]

Making the industry responsible for these kinds of incidents is an example of paternalism—that is, treating Americans like little children who have to be taken care of by the parent, in this case the gun industry. But the vast majority of people who use guns are adults. They don't need to be supervised and taken care of by the government or by manufacturers. For the minority of gun users who are not adults, their own parents should be supervising them, not the courts or an industrial substitute parent.

The lawsuits against the gun industry are being based on two improper kinds of arguments: that gun manufacturers haven't kept their products from getting into the hands of criminals, and that guns are inherently dangerous.

It is not the responsibility of gun makers to keep track of everyone who buys one of their products. No other industry has to do this even though there are many products that cause far more deaths and injuries than guns do. More people die from poison than from guns. More people are injured by someone wielding a baseball bat than are hurt with guns. Should the makers of those products, too, be required to keep track of all of their customers? Can you imagine any industry being required to do that?

First of all, this kind of notion is utterly impractical. With 1.5 million guns sold in the United States each year, how could anyone possibly keep track of all those sales? Second, if it *could* be done, it would be a terrible infringement on Americans' right to privacy. Why should a company—or the government—have records about the kinds of things people buy? Many gun owners fear that this kind of tracking would lead to harassment by law enforcement officials.

As for the argument that guns are dangerous—of course guns can be dangerous! But used correctly, they can be useful tools for sport and for self-defense. As Robert W. Tracinski, editor of the *Intellectual Activist*, writes, "A gun is a tool. If a person uses that tool responsibly, it poses a danger only to criminals [when used for self-defense]. It is the gun owner's choice—not [its] mere existence . . . , and not its manufacture and sale—that determines its use."[5]

Ridiculous Lawsuits

The United States is known for its ridiculous lawsuits. People spill hot coffee in their lap and they sue McDonald's. They smoke for twenty-five years, despite well-publicized warnings about the health dangers, then they get cancer and they sue the cigarette makers. They stop taking the medicine that controls their mental illness, they do something crazy, and they sue their doctors.

Now people are going into league to try to squeeze every penny they can out of the gun industry by blaming society's problems on guns. This is ridiculous. As Tracinski writes,

> Liability law ought to be based on the principles of individual responsibility: the idea that an individual is liable for harm caused by his own actions. But the suit against the gun manufacturers seeks to shift this responsibility to an inanimate object [the gun] and to its manufacturer. . . . There are no limits to the suits that could be brought under this standard.[6]

There is even a large group of lawyers working together to focus on putting the gun industry out of business. This group of forty law firms is called the Castano Group and is led by personal-injury lawyer Wendell Gauthier. Gauthier boasted in a televised press conference, "We're a bad dream for the gun industry."[7] Gauthier says the group's plan "is to get so many lawyers to launch so many lawsuits so fast in so many places that the firearms industry simply splinters and disintegrates."[8]

The sad fact is that this despicable tactic may work. The lawyers may have more resources than the gun industry. By filing hundreds of lawsuits, they can stretch the gun industry's legal resources so thin that they will be ineffective. "Even if we win the suits, the expense of fighting means we lose,"[9] said a spokesperson for the American Shooting Sports Council.

If these lawsuits go forward, not only the gun industry but also America will be in trouble. As an article in *American Rifleman* magazine says, "Losing this tidal wave of lawsuits means gun ownership will be unaffordable. And a Second Amendment Americans cannot afford to exercise is no Second Amendment at all."[10] If Americans can no longer afford to buy guns, they will no longer be able to defend the country in an emergency, nor will they be able to defend themselves if the government starts taking away other rights.

Can Laws Save Guns?

Several states have written laws forbidding these wholesale, frivolous suits against gun makers. All Americans should hope these laws work. Lawsuits designed to badger an industry to death are not the democratic way. Newspaper columnist D.J. Tice points out, "Courts exist to apply laws made through [the democratic process]. When they are used to punish what the

democratic process has deliberately left legal, a crime against freedom itself has been committed."[11]

If Americans truly want guns to disappear from U.S. society, then they should work to get the laws changed. But the truth is that Americans want guns. Almost half of all American homes contain at least one gun, and people buy a million and a half new guns every year. This doesn't sound like a country that doesn't want guns.

It is only a virulent minority that is trying to get their own way by going after the gun industry. Because they don't have enough support from the American people, they have failed to get laws passed banning guns. Now they're trying to do it "through the back door." They think they can run the gun manufacturers out of business by getting courts to hold them responsible for careless and criminal gun use. Their tactic is wrong. It is undemocratic. It is un-American. Gun makers are no more responsible for the wrong use of their products than baseball bat manufacturers are.

1. Quoted in J.D. Tuccille, "High Noon in the Courtroom," January 24, 1999. http://civiliberty.about.com.

2. David Firestone, "Georgia Bill Aims to Block Anti-Gun Lawsuits," *New York Times*, February 9, 1999, p. A1.

3. Quoted in James Pilcher, "NRA Aims to Head Off Anti-Firearm Litigation," *St. Paul Pioneer Press*, February 5, 1999.

4. Jack Lenning, letter, *St. Paul Pioneer Press*, March 4, 1999, p. 10A.

5. Robert W. Tracinski, "An Unjust Assault on Guns," Ayn Rand Institute. www.aynrand.org/medialink/guns.shtml.

6. Tracinski, "An Unjust Assault on Guns."

7. Quoted in *American Rifleman*, "Hired Guns Aim for Your Guns," May 1999, p. 44.

8. Quoted in *American Rifleman*, "Hired Guns Aim for Your Guns," p. 44.

9. Quoted in Jacob Sullum, "Nuisance Suits," *Reason Online*, November 18, 1998. www.reasonmag.com/sullum/111898.html.

10. *American Rifleman*, "Hired Guns Aim for Your Guns," p. 46.

11. D. J. Tice, "Opinion," *St. Paul Pioneer Press*, February 18, 1999.

CHAPTER 4

How Would a Gun Ban Affect Society?

"[Hunting is] more than a sport. It's a way of life and a heritage."

Banning Guns Would Harm Society

When I was six years old, my father took me along as he hunted deer; he showed me how to walk quietly, to move along and then to stop and listen carefully before taking another step. A year later, he traded a pistol for a little single-shot .22 rifle just my size.

He took me and my younger sisters down to the dump by the river and taught us how to shoot. We rummaged through the trash for bottles and glass jars; it was great fun to take aim at a pickle jar and watch it shatter. If the Rio San Jose had water running in it, we threw bottles for moving targets in the muddy current. My father told us that a .22 bullet can travel a mile, so we had to be careful where we aimed. The river was a good place because it was below the villages and away from the houses; the high clay riverbanks wouldn't let any bullets stray. Gun safety was drilled into us. . . . Guns were not toys.[1]

Novelist Leslie Marmon Silko, quoted above, describes the experience of many Americans who grew up knowing guns and viewing them as both recreational and utilitarian tools. Silko is a Laguna Pueblo Indian. During her childhood in the 1950s and 1960s, her father and others in her community routinely hunted as part of their means of filling the family pantry. In other American communities, too, hunting was—and still is—a way of life. In fact, 16 to 18 million Americans hunt on a regular basis.

Tom Gamble, a hunter from Wellsboro, Pennsylvania, told a National Public Radio (NPR) reporter, "To me, it's more than a sport. It's a way of life and a heritage. My son—I've had him in the woods with me since he was old enough to walk. And I just want to see other children, you know, experience the same things that he and I have." Another Wellsboro hunter, Joe Davis, agrees: "It's the one thing that you can bond with your father."[2]

Hunting in the Classroom

NPR profiled the little community of Idaho City, Idaho, a town of about three hundred people, nearly all of whom own and use guns. Bob Bash, the town's elementary school principal, told the NPR reporter that he "has a passion for hunting, which he's passed on to his sons and students. . . . He grew up hunting, and that's what he knows and loves."[3] In fact, Bash teaches three hunter education and firearm safety courses, including a hands-on class in the elementary school.

Some people say that there are too many guns in this country, but according to Idaho City teacher Susan Caywood, "I think the answer to that is, if you have guns around, just as you have automobiles, you have alcohol, you have drugs, you need to teach responsibility and respect."[4] If more people had this attitude, society might have fewer problems with guns.

Paul Forester also teaches hunter safety classes in Idaho City. He points out that there are still some places in the United States where guns are needed for everyday safety. Forester used to live in Alaska, a state still filled with wilderness. He objects to people who live in cities making rules for people who live in places like that. Forester says, "Some guy's talking about gun control, when he's sitting in his Manhattan highrise, going around and around Central Park, that is going to affect a guy who lives in Kodiak, Alaska, and has to walk to an outhouse to go take a pee, right? There's bears and there's whatever, and he's telling him he can't have a gun in his house."[5]

Banning guns would be very unfair to people like these, people who use guns for their safety and livelihood.

Gun Hobbyists

There are also people for whom guns are a hobby. "Many people keep firearms just for the joy of looking at them. Much like classic cars or old cameras, custom guns are finely crafted instruments. Working on them or shooting them is a matter of enjoying the process the way fishermen or music lovers do,"[6] says Oleg Volk, a young photographer who enjoys firearms. Collectors should not be robbed of their right to have guns just because a few criminals misuse these instruments.

Some people become gun collectors because of their love of history. They learn more about the Revolutionary War or

Some people collect guns because of their significance in American history.

the frontier expansion by collecting firearms of the period or by attending or participating in reenactments of the events. "Can you imagine America without a Colt, Remington, or Winchester? Our guns explored continents, opened the West, secured freedom, won wars, and preserved peace. Guns make law enforcemnent possible,"[7] said a writer in *American Rifleman*, a magazine published by the National Rifle Association.

Go to any historical battlefield, like Gettysburg in Pennsylvania, where some of our nation's most decisive moments occurred, and you'll find elaborate reenactments of the battles and the lifestyles of the time. Gun lovers, history buffs, and actors join together in a harmless form of living education more vivid than any textbook. Volk says, "Arms, be they Kentucky rifles that ushered in the Revolution of 1776, percussion six-guns that won the West, or submachine guns used to defeat the Nazis, are part of our cultural heritage. Elimination of collectors' guns does nothing to keep thugs . . . from abusing the weapons they have."[8]

Competiton

Many people enjoy competitive shooting sports. Even the Olympics has competitive shooting events. People involved in these sports must do much more than aim and fire. There are many skills involved. To do well in the National Rifle Association's Youth Hunter Education competition, for example, the entrants' "shooting must be dead-on with muzzle-loaders, .22s, shotguns, as well as archery and a written test on hunter safety and wildlife identification."[9]

No one need fear young people involved in this kind of shooting activity. Safety is a vital part of all such programs. As Bob Bash says,

> For our kids out here that have grown up with guns, we just don't understand [incidents like school shooting rampages]. . . .Why would they ever take

something that we hold dear as a tool, why would they take that and use that as a weapon against another student? See, it would be as foreign to folks who are in a baseball community that grew up with baseball to take a baseball bat and bludgeon one of their classmates.[10]

A Misguided Approach

"Just like those who play golf recreationally," says Oleg Volk, "shooters hit clays [flying targets] or pop cans while chatting with friends."[11] There's nothing wrong with innocent pastimes like this, and it would be wrong to deprive people of such pleasures in a misguided effort to end violence in this country. It's not the plinkers, hunters, and collectors who cause violence, nor is the fact that guns exist the reason for American violence. Those who want to ban guns should stop and take a look at the real impact this would have on crime, firearm accidents, and suicides—very little. It would be better to encourage gun aficionados to share their interest with others and to encourage gun safety and appreciation.

1. Leslie Marmon Silko, "In the Combat Safety Zone," *Hungry Mind Review*, September 1, 1995.

2. Quoted in National Public Radio, "Gun Control Series," *Morning Edition*, June 15, 1999.

3. Elizabeth Arnold, "Gun Control Series," *Morning Edition*, National Public Radio, June 16, 1999.

4. Quoted in Arnold, "Gun Control Series."

5. Quoted in Arnold, "Gun Control Series."

6. Oleg Volk, "Guns as Fine Art." www.ddb.com/olegv/guns/fineart.html.

7. *American Rifleman*, "Hired Guns Take Aim at Your Guns," May 1999.

8. Volk, "Guns as Fine Art."

9. Larry Abramson, "Gun Control Series," *Morning Edition*, National Public Radio, June 18, 1999.

10. Quoted in Arnold, "Gun Control Series."

11. Volk, "Guns as Fine Art."

"Violence has accompanied virtually every stage and aspect of our national existence . . . [and] it has been a determinant of both the form and substance of American life."

Banning Guns Would Not Solve America's Problem with Violence

Even if it were possible to ban guns—several hundred million are in private hands right now[1]—that would not end the violence. Face it: America was born in violence, and violence is at the heart of the American soul. To change that, a lot more is needed than destroying a few guns.

Guns in American History and Myth

The United States was born in the violence of revolution. Historian Richard Maxwell Brown writes, "Violence has accompanied virtually every stage and aspect of our national existence . . . [and] it has been a determinant of both the form and substance of American life. We have resorted so often to violence that we have long since become a trigger-happy people."[2]

Guns were essential tools in every household during colonial times, both for fighting the British and for procuring game for food. As the nation expanded, it did so with the help of guns that fought off hostile Indians—or helped steal the

85

land of others. Frontier people like the colonists needed their guns not only for fighting but also for protection from animals and enemies and for getting food. Guns were essential tools, but they also became romantic symbols.

American folklore is filled with heroes and villains whose "magic wand" is their gun, and often the villains have become the "heroes" of American mythology. Psychologist Jonathan Kellerman points out that

> American history and folklore are rich with examples of bad kids blazing their way across the plains. Jesse James was seventeen years old when he rode with Quantrill's Confederate guerillas—a gang of murderous psychopaths that justified its viciousness with paramilitary rhetoric. By the age of nineteen, James had committed his first murder. William H. Bonney—Billy the Kid—was even more precocious, slaying his first victim at the tender age of fourteen. By his twenty-first birthday he'd left twenty-one dead men behind. Butch Cassidy began rustling cattle during early adolecence and graduated to robbing trains before he was twenty. . . .
>
> The fact that American folklore has lionized the likes of Billy the Kid, Jesse James, and [the murderous bank robbers] Bonnie and Clyde, elevating them to folk heroes, combined with our general glorification of the brutal and violent periods such as the Wild West, may tell us something about our true feelings toward youthful murderousness.[3]

The United States still often acts out its romantic vision of the Western myth. Americans tend to think that problems can be solved with firepower. For at least the past century, it has been common practice for the United States to ride in, guns blazing, to solve other nations' problems. Teddy Roosevelt led the charge in the Spanish-American War; Dwight Eisenhower

American folklore has made heroes of such gun-toting criminals as Butch Cassidy (pictured, lower right).

led it in the Korean conflict of the 1950s; Ronald Reagan led it in the tiny island nation of Grenada in 1983. These are only three of a dozen or so examples from twentieth-century American history, and it doesn't look like the American impulse to "shoot first, ask questions later" is likely to change as the world moves into a new millennium.

"In short, [some observers say,] we are still too close to our gun-soaked past to entertain seriously the idea of giving up our guns,"[4] writes historian Gregg Lee Carter.

Americans, Guns, and Violence

Americans are addicted to guns and violence. There are other countries with almost as many guns per person as the United States, but they have dramatically smaller numbers of gun deaths. Interpol, an international law enforcement organization, collects crime statistics from all over the world. Interpol's findings show that in Norway, for example, a third of the country's households have one or more guns. But there are only three firearm murders and thirty-nine firearm suicides for every million people in Norway, while the United States has forty-six firearm murders and seventy-three firearm suicides. In Canada, too, a third of all households have guns. But for every million people, Canada has only seven firearm murders and four firearm suicides.

The United States is different from most other nations. It has one of the highest rates of firearms violence in the world. The few nations that have more gun deaths and crime than the United States are countries in a state of war, whether political (South Africa), economic (Russia), or criminal (Colombia and its drug wars). William Weir, author of *A Well-Regulated Militia*, identifies several factors that make the United States unusual and help perpetuate its gun culture:

• *Social diversity.* Of the countries Weir examined, the more peaceful ones tend to have more homogeneous populations. That is, the vast majority of people have similar cultural backgrounds. Japan, for example, has a culture that is shared by most of its people. The United States, on the other hand, is made up of people from hundreds of different cultural backgrounds with varied beliefs and customs that are often in conflict with one another.

• *Social instability.* Weir found that the citizens of more peaceful nations often have little mobility. People live and work in the same place and often in the same ways as their parents and grandparents. Extended families live together and help maintain the family's—and the country's—core values. Greece, with only five firearm murders and eight firearm suicides per million people, is a good example. In the United States, typically it is only the immediate family that lives together, and often that family has only one parent. Other relatives may live in the same city or may be spread around the country. Additionally, people change both homes and jobs frequently.

• *Economic inequality.* More peaceful countries have fewer economic extremes. The incomes of the poorest and the wealthiest people are much closer together than in the United States. Even in poorer countries, most people are poor together. The United States, on the other hand, has as many economic extremes as cultural ones. America has the world's largest number of billionaires, but it also has many areas of extreme poverty as well as a huge middle class. As newspaper writer Brian Toogood describes it, any country that is "a competitive, individualistic, 'winner take all' free-market society that generates as many 'losers' as ours can count on those outcasts to erupt occasionally in violent retaliation. It is inevitable."[5]

• *Envy.* Weir calls this the Tantalus Syndrome. In the Greek myth, Tantalus is punished by the gods by being confined in a well with water up to his neck. He's perishing of thirst, but when he tries to drink, the water drains away. Delicious fruits hang over his head, but he can't reach them. He is *tantalized* by what he can't have. American society is like that. Commercials, billboards, television programs, movies, and other information sources shout from all sides about expensive luxuries that are available, but only if one has the money to buy them. The "have-nots" are naturally envious of the wealth and luxury they see around them. They want a share in the American dream, too. Often, this envy results in violence.

Inevitable Violence

When you take America's frontier heritage and combine it with today's social and economic inequities, violence becomes almost inevitable. Unless Americans can deglamorize outlaws and create a better social and economic balance, getting rid of guns will have little impact on America's violent society.

---

1. Each year, about 1.5 million new guns are sold. There are 80 million registered gun owners and untold numbers of nonregistered owners. Many owners who are collectors literally own hundreds of firearms and many noncollectors own dozens, in much the same way woodworking hobbyists own dozens of tools.

2. Quoted in Gregg Lee Carter, *The Gun Control Movement*. New York: Twayne, 1997, p. 36.

3. Jonathan Kellerman, *Savage Spawn: Reflections on Violent Children*. New York: Ballantine, 1999, pp. 100–101.

4. Carter, *The Gun Control Movement*, p. 36.

5. Brian Toogood, "Some Dangers Unavoidable, but One Emphatically Isn't," *St. Paul Pioneer Press*, June 6, 1999.

"Just prohibit the blood-drenched things!"

Banning Guns Would Help Reduce the Level of Violence in Society

Knowing about the horrifying numbers of people who are injured and killed in America each day by guns can lead any thinking person to only one conclusion: America must ban guns.

Guns are the most frequent cause of death for young black and Hispanic men. In 1994 guns were the second most frequent cause of death for white youths. They are used in more than 2,000 crimes each day in this country. In 1993 guns were the most frequent cause of injury-related deaths in California and five other states. In addition, experts estimate that three times more people are wounded by firearms than are killed—that's around 135,000 firearms injuries in 1995 alone. In 1995 the United States had the highest rate of firearm suicides of all of the wealthier nations in the world. In 1996 New Zealand had only 2 handgun murders, Japan had 15, Great Britain had 30, Canada had 106, Germany had 213—and the United States had 9,390.

Guns Contribute to America's Culture of Violence

People say that it would be difficult to ban guns; they are a part of our heritage. Guns "opened" the American West. But never in American history have guns been used to create so much tragedy as they do today. In fact, historian Eugene Hollon makes this astounding statement: "The Western frontier was a far more civilized, more peaceful, and safer place than American society today."[1]

Yet the myth of the violent Old West is passed on through books, movies, television, and games—and not just the ones actually set in the West. Old West mythology is the basis for most of the "shoot-'em-ups" that Americans view as entertainment. First Lady Hillary Clinton notes,

> When our culture romaticizes violence and glorifies violence on TV, in the movies, on the Internet, in songs, and when there are video games that you win based on how many people you kill, then I think the evidence is absolutely clear—our children become desensitized to violence and lose their empathy for fellow human beings. Studies show what many of us have believed, that such exposure causes more aggression and antisocial behavior. . . . America's culture of violence is having a profound effect on our children, and we must resolve to do what we can to change that culture.[2]

Every time a major incident of violence occurs, people are quick to blame the media's influence. People point to movies, television, video games, and popular music as influencing society in unhealthy ways. But it's not enough to blame the media for glamorizing violence. After the 1999 shooting tragedy in Littleton, Colorado, newspaper columnist Laura Billings wrote,

> We do the usual things by calling for more school security and shaming Hollywood for supplying our appetite for violent images. Teenagers across the country are signing pointless pledges that they won't bring guns to school, while anxious parents are

boosting sales of software that limits their children's access to the Internet. We feel we are doing something, without, of course, doing anything at all to challenge an American mindset that regards the Second Amendment as though it were handed down on a stone tablet.[3]

What we have to do is change that mindset and get rid of guns. Columnist Denis Horgan insists, "We can change. We know that we have in our laws the skeleton key to mayhem and mothers crying out in anguish."[4] That key is guns. Even as efforts are taking place to tone down violence in the media or to assign various kinds of ratings systems, we must go right to the cause—guns—and treat it like we would treat the cause of any disease—eliminate it.

Great Britain Bans Handguns

It can be done. In 1997 England banned semiautomatic weapons (guns that can shoot several bullets in quick succession) and handguns, and it forbade keeping guns in private homes. The gun banning was prompted by a 1996 tragedy in which a Scottish scout master massacred sixteen nursery-school children and their teachers. In response to outrage over the incident, the British government forbade further manufacturing or importing of these lethal weapons, and it demanded that people who owned such guns give them up. It bought some two hundred thousand guns from its citizens and then destroyed the weapons. Remarkably little protest was raised.

Unlike England, America doesn't seem to learn from its tragedies. Incidents like the school shooting in Littleton, Colorado, and horrifying daily fatality statistics that come out of impoverished city pockets inspire some debate but little real action. A British magazine notes, "Of all rich countries, only America makes it possible for teenage misfits, those nursing a grudge, the insane, or anyone else determined to cause mayhem to get their hands so easily on such a terrifying weapon."[5]

Banning handguns should be the first step in the United States. Handguns are far and away the most often used weapons in crimes, murders, and suicides. They are easy to carry, easy to conceal, and easy to cause harm. They are not intended for hunting, so hunters have no good reason to have them. They're not good for protection; studies repeatedly show that "people who keep guns in the home for self-protection place themselves and their families at risk."[6] What they are good for is hurting and killing people.

England allows people to own hunting rifles and competition guns, but they must be stored safely away from the home—like at a gun club. If Americans feel there's a need to keep this kind of gun sport going, we could set the same kind of rules: No guns in the home; no guns at all that aren't carefully locked away under responsible supervision.

If the country did this, crime of all sorts would soon decrease to a manageable level. People would no longer have to be afraid to take an evening walk. The United States could truly become once again the land of the free.

Taking Responsibility

The United States must get started on this essential goal: Make people see the danger of guns and get rid of them. It won't be easy—violence is embedded in American society. Yet the enormity of the problem should not be used as an excuse for complacency. As President Bill Clinton notes, "Cultures are hard to change. [But] cultures should never be used to avoid individual responsibility."[7] Before a recent gathering of gun-control experts, the president summed up the most pragmatic approach to changing America's violent, gun-obsessed culture: "You change the culture, we'll change the laws."[8]

The dangers of tobacco have been heavily publicized, resulting in a decrease in smoking and tougher regulation of cigarettes. The same kind of campaign should be waged against guns: Publicize their dangers, enforce the laws that already exist, then follow newspaper columnist Denis Horgan's advice: "Just prohibit the blood-drenched things!"[9]

1. Quoted in Gregg Lee Carter, *The Gun Control Movement*, New York: Twayne, 1997, p. 47.

2. Hillary Clinton, remarks on gun-control legislation. Washington, DC: Office of the White House, April 27, 1999.

3. Laura Billings, "What Everyone Sees—Except in the U.S.," *St. Paul Pioneer Press*, May 5, 1999.

4. Denis Horgan, "Forget Haphazard, Halfhearted Gun 'Control' and Dump Second Amendment Outright," *St. Paul Pioneer Press*, May 21, 1999.

5. Quoted in Billings, "What Everyone Sees—Except in the U.S."

6. Coalition to Stop Gun Violence, "Unintentional Shootings." www.gunfree.org/csgv/bsc_uni.htm.

7. Bill Clinton, remarks on gun-control legislation, Washington, DC: Office of the White House, April 27, 1999.

8. Bill Clinton, remarks to gun-control advocates at a White House conference following the Littleton, Colorado, school massacre. Washington, DC: Office of the White House, May 27, 1999.

9. Horgan, "Forget Haphazard, Halfhearted Gun 'Control' and Dump Second Amendment Outright."

STUDY QUESTIONS

Chapter 1

1. After reading these viewpoints, do you think guns are more harmful or more helpful? List three facts that you find especially convincing.

2. Do you think laws that make it harder for kids to get guns would decrease school violence? Would they decrease other juvenile crime? Explain your answer.

3. Jonathan Kellerman, quoted in viewpoint 4, says that some kids are just bad; that there's something essentially wrong with them. Explain why you agree or disagree with this idea.

Chapter 2

1. After reading the viewpoints in this chapter, do you think the U.S. Constitution supports the right of everyone to own guns? List two factors mentioned in the viewpoints that support your view.

2. Newspaper columnist Denis Horgan says, "Dump the Second Amendment." He says it is outdated and no longer suits our society. Forget for the moment your own beliefs about guns and gun control. Do you think it would be right to "dump" part of the Constitution? Explain.

Chapter 3

1. At what age do you think people should be able to buy guns? Give reasons for your answer.

2. Viewpoint 1 recommends several laws to reduce gun violence. Which laws would you support? Which do you think are a bad idea? Explain your answer.

3. Do you think crimes involving guns should be punished more severely than others? Why or why not?

4. Do you think lawsuits against gun manufacturers, like those discussed in viewpoints 3 and 4, are a good or bad idea? Why?

5. Independence and self-reliance are traits often identified as particularly American. Some people say the idea of suing gun companies goes against the grain of these traits. Explain why you agree or disagree with this view.

Chapter 4

1. Do you think there's value to allowing people to use guns for sport—hunting and competitive shooting, for example? Explain.

2. Do you think that banning guns would significantly reduce violence in America? Explain.

3. Viewpoint 2 suggests that violence is an inherent part of the American character. Do you agree or disagree with this idea? If you agree, do you think that trait can be changed? How?

General

1. There are several charts and lists of statistics in this book showing how the United States has a much higher incidence of violence involving guns than most other industrialized nations. What do you think is the significance of this? Is it something the United States needs to work to change? Explain your answer.

2. What is your position on gun control? In what ways, if any, should guns and gun ownership be regulated by the government? What gun-control measures would you consider reasonable and responsible?

APPENDIX A

Facts About Gun Control

- The *1995 Annual Firearms Manufacturing and Export Report*, published by the Bureau of Alcohol, Tobacco, and Firearms, reports that almost 1.8 million guns were manufactured in the United States that year. The top ten manufacturers produced 1.5 million of them.

- Americans buy 1.4 million new guns each year.

- In 1995 Tulane University criminologist James Wright told a congressional subcommittee that there are more than 200 million firearms in circulation in the United States today.

- The *Canadian Medical Association Journal* reported in 1993 that of fifteen countries, the United States had the highest percentage of households with one or more guns (48 percent). The next highest rates were in Norway, where 32 percent of households had one or more guns; Canada, 29 percent; and Switzerland, 27 percent. The United States had about 12 gun murders and suicides per 100,000 people, Norway had about 3.3, Canada had about 4.5, and Switzerland had about 6.2.

- The Center to Prevent Handgun Violence reports that 50 percent of the Americans who keep guns in their homes keep them loaded.

- The Gun Owners Foundation reports that at least 17 million American women own firearms.

- The National Opinion Research Center at the University of Illinois reported in a 1998 survey that:
  - Nearly one out of ten adults says that he or she has carried a handgun away from home during the last year.
  - Thirty-four percent of gun owners purchased their guns at a store that specializes in gun sales; 18.6 percent bought them from a department store, sporting goods store, or other store that sells other kinds of merchandise as well as guns; 6.1 percent purchased them at pawnshops; 1.7 percent ordered them through the mail; 10.6 percent bought them from a friend; 11.8 percent received them as a gift; 9.7 percent inherited them; 2 percent bought them at gun shows.

Guns and Crime

The Gun Owners Foundation reports that:

- People use guns as many as 2.5 million times every year to defend themselves (about 6,850 times per day), and in the majority of these incidents, the gun owner merely shows the weapon and doesn't actually shoot it.
- Since Florida legalized the right to carry a concealed handgun in 1987, more than 380,000 people have obtained permits, and Florida's murder rate has fallen 36 percent.
- A 1996 study found that states that made it legal to carry concealed handguns had a significant drop in crime (murder rates went down 8.5 percent; rapes down 5 percent; aggravated assaults down 7 percent; and robbery down 3 percent).
- Statistical comparisons with other countries show that burglars in the United States are far less likely to enter an occupied home than burglars in countries with fewer privately owned firearms.
- Ninety-three percent of felons acquired their guns illegally.
- Violent criminals carry assault weapons in only about 1 percent of their crimes.
- An FBI report states that in a confrontation, a person has a much greater chance of being killed by a knife than by any kind of rifle.
- Sixty-one percent of gun murder victims have criminal records.
- The Bureau of Justice Statistics reported in 1993 that out of all violent crimes, only 10 percent of the perpetrators used guns.
- John R. Lott Jr., author of *More Guns, Less Crime*, states that women are two and a half times more likely to suffer injury from an attacker if they do not resist than if they resist with a gun.
- The National Center for Policy Analysis reports that only 0.09 percent of all the guns owned in America are used in the commission of crimes.

Gun-Related Deaths

- The *Los Angeles Times* reported that there were more than thirty-four thousand gun deaths in the United States in 1996. These include murders, suicides, and accidents.

According to the *International Journal of Epidemiology*, out of thirty-seven countries surveyed in 1993–1994:

- The United States ranked fifth highest in the per capita number of firearm murders (4.61 gun murders for every 100,000 people). Only Estonia, Brazil, Mexico, and Northern Ireland had higher rates.

- Guns are the weapon used in one-third of all U.S. murders.

- The United States ranked fourth highest in total murder rate (6.8 per 100,000), behind Estonia (28.21), Brazil (19.04), and Mexico (17.58).

- The countries with the lowest rates of gun murders are Mauritius (none), the Republic of Ireland (only 3 per 10 million people), and England/Wales (7 per 10 million people).

The same study showed that:

- The United States had the highest per capita rate of firearm suicides (7.35 suicides for every 100,000 people). The countries with the next highest rates were Finland (5.78), Switzerland (5.61), and France (5.14).

- Guns are used in 60 percent of U.S. suicides.

- The United States ranked twentieth in total suicides (12.06 per 100,000 people).

- The countries with the lowest rates of gun suicides are South Korea (2 per 10 million people), Japan (4 per 10 million), and Kuwait (6 per 10 million).

- The National Health Safety Council ranked firearms as the eighth highest cause of accidental deaths in the United States in 1997 (1,500 deaths). The highest causes were car accidents (43,200), falls (14,900), and poisoning (8,600).

- The Violence Policy Center reports that in a study of 352 murders of women, almost all of the murder victims (89 percent) were killed by someone they knew, and more than half (54 percent) were killed with guns.

Federal Gun Laws

- In a June 1999 speech, President Bill Clinton reported that between 1994 and 1999 the Brady Handgun Control Act had prevented four hundred thousand sales of guns to people with criminal convictions or records of domestic abuse, drug abuse, or mental illness.

State Gun Laws

- There are more than twenty thousand state laws governing gun ownership, handling, and use.

The National Rifle Association's 1998 Compendium of State Laws Governing Firearms shows that:

- Tennessee and Connecticut had the longest waiting period for buying guns from licensed dealers. In Tennessee the wait was fifteen days; in Connecticut it was fourteen days. Thirty-one states had no waiting period at all.
- Only six states required registration of all newly purchased guns.
- Thirty-one states had either no laws or fairly liberal laws regarding concealed guns.
- Eight states had laws against carrying concealed guns.

Data from the National Center for Health Statistics shows how the states rank in number of firearm-related deaths in 1995:

- The District of Columbia had by far the highest rate: 30.1 per 100,000 people. These were all murders—34 of them.
- California had the highest number of gun murders (365), but ranked eleventh highest (along with Maryland and Missouri) in per capita gun deaths (5.6 per 100,000 people). Texas had the second highest number of gun murders (171) and a per capita rate of 5.1 per 100,000.
- California also led the nation in gun suicides (77) and accidental gun deaths (39).
- The states with the highest rate of gun deaths per 100,000 people were Arkansas (8.7), Mississippi (8.4), Arizona (7.6), Louisiana (7.5), and Alabama (7.1).
- The states with the lowest rate of gun deaths per 100,000 people were Rhode Island (0.9), Hawaii (1.0), Massachusetts (1.2), New Jersey (1.6), Maine (1.7), and Connecticut (2.0).

Firearm Violence Involving Children and/or Schools

The May 3, 1999, issue of *Newsweek* reported that:

- In 1997, 8 percent of high school students said they had carried a weapon to school in the preceding month.

- Forty-three percent of the nation's schools reported no crime at all in the 1996–1997 school year, and the incidents that were reported were mostly minor crimes.
- Since 1992 the annual death toll from school shootings has ranged from twenty to fifty-five.
- Fewer than 1 percent of gun deaths involving school-age children occur in or around schools.
- The Center to Prevent Handgun Violence reports that a study of accidental shootings involving children under sixteen showed that nearly 40 percent of the incidents happened in the homes of friends and relatives, not on the street.
- The Center for the Study and Prevention of Violence reports that male school-age children have a 7.3 times greater risk of fatal and 6.0 times greater risk of nonfatal firearms injuries than female children.

Public Opinion Regarding Guns and Gun Control

A 1998 survey conducted by the National Opinion Research Center at the University of Chicago found that:

- Two-thirds of gun owners and 80 percent of the general public favor mandatory background checks in private gun sales.
- Three-fourths of gun owners and 85 percent of the general public support mandatory handgun registration.
- Eighty-three percent of the public believe that public places such as restaurants, theaters, and stores should be gun free.
- Seventy-one percent say they would be willing to pay twenty-five dollars in additional taxes to reduce gun injuries.
- Ninety percent believe all gun buyers should take a gun-safety course.
- Of those polled, 87.9 percent believe all new handguns should be made childproof.
- The survey revealed that 79.6 percent of the public believes that gun owners should be required to store guns in a manner that makes them inaccessible to children.
- Fifteen percent say they would like to see a total ban on handguns.

Appendix B

Excerpts from Related Documents

Document 1: International Violent Death Rates

When considering the question of gun control, it is often useful to compare the United States to other countries. The following chart shows how the number of violent deaths in the United States compares to the violent deaths in other countries classified as "higher-income nations" by the World Bank. From this chart, one can calculate the percentage that involve guns.

Guncite, "International Violent Death Rates," June 25, 1999. www.guncite.com/gcgvintl.html.

Country	Year	Population	Total Death	Total Homicide	Firearm Homicide	Total Suicide	Firearm Suicide	Percentage of Households with Guns
Finland	1994	5,088,333	30.72	3.24	0.86	27.26	5.78	23.2
Denmark	1993	5,189,378	23.46	1.21	0.23	22.13	2.25	n/a
Austria	1994	8,029,717	23.36	1.17	0.42	22.12	4.06	n/a
Switzerland[1]	1994	7,021,000	22.80	1.32	0.58	21.28	5.61	27.2
France	1994	57,915,450	22.67	1.12	0.44	20.79	5.14	22.6
Belgium	1990	9,967,387	20.77	1.41	0.60	19.04	2.56	16.6
United States[2]	1993	257,783,004	18.86	6.80	4.61	12.06	7.35	48.0
Japan	1994	124,069,000	17.34	0.62	0.02	16.72	0.04	n/a
Sweden	1993	8,718,571	17.12	1.30	0.18	15.75	2.09	15.1
Germany[3]	1994	81,338,093	17.00	1.17	0.22	15.64	1.17	8.9
Taiwan[4]	1996	21,979,444	15.00	8.12	0.97	6.88	0.12	n/a
Singapore	1994	2,930,200	15.77	1.71	0.07	14.06	0.17	n/a
Canada	1992	28,120,065	15.64	2.16	0.76	13.19	3.72	29.1
Norway	1993	4,324,815	14.75	0.97	0.30	13.64	3.95	32.0
N. Ireland	1994	1,641,711	14.74	6.09	5.24	8.41	1.34	8.4
Australia	1994	17,838,401	14.65	1.86	0.44	12.65	2.35	19.4
New Zealand	1993	3,458,850	14.63	1.47	0.17	12.81	2.14	22.3
Scotland	1994	5,132,400	14.46	2.24	0.19	12.16	0.31	4.7
Hong Kong	1993	5,919,000	11.52	1.23	0.12	10.29	0.07	n/a
Netherlands	1994	15,382,830	11.25	1.11	0.36	10.10	0.31	1.9
Ireland	1991	3,525,719	10.68	0.62	0.03	9.81	0.94	n/a
Italy	1992	56,764,854	10.42	2.25	1.66	8.00	1.11	16.0
England/Wales	1992	51,429,000	8.28	0.55	0.07	7.68	0.33	4.7
Israel	1993	5,261,700	9.80	2.32	0.72	7.05	1.84	n/a
Spain	1993	39,086,079	8.97	0.95	0.21	7.77	0.43	13.1
Kuwait	1995	1,684,529	3.50	1.01	0.36	1.66	0.06	n/a

Notes:

1. Percent households with guns includes all army personnel.

2. Total homicide rate and firearm homicide rates are from *FBI Uniform Crime Report (1997)*. (The FBI reports homicides fell to 6.2 per 100,000 in 1998).

3. Percent households with guns excludes eastern Germany.

4. Number of homicides: Ministry of Interior, National Police Administration, Taiwan.

   Population: As of April 1999, Government Information Office, Taiwan.

   Gun Homicides: Central News Agency, Taipei, November 23, 1997.

   Sources: The first eight columns of data are from the International Journal of Epidemiology 1998:27:216. The "Total Death" column was calculated by including homicides, suicides, and unintentional and undetermined firearm (not shown here) rates.

Document 2: Student Pledge Against Gun Violence

Following a highly publicized school gun tragedy in 1996, a group of Minnesota students decided to do something about the violence that seemed to be overtaking their generation. They composed a pledge, which is reprinted below, and began a campaign to have students all over the country sign and follow it.

I will never bring a gun to school; I will never use a gun to settle a dispute; I will use my influence with my friends to keep them from using guns to settle disputes.

My individual choices and actions, when multiplied by those of young people throughout the country, will make a difference. Together, by honoring this pledge, we can reverse the violence and grow up in safety.

Student Pledge Against Gun Violence, "I Pledge." www.pledge.org.

Document 3: Handguns and Self-Defense

Many people own guns for self-defense. In the following excerpt from a Fall 1993 article in Public Interest, *author Jeffrey R. Snyder contends that handguns are vital to individuals' efforts to protect themselves from crime.*

The media and the law enforcement establishment continually advise us that, when confronted with the threat of lethal violence, we should not resist, but simply give the attacker what he wants. If the crime under consideration is rape, there is some notable waffling on this point, and the discussion quickly moves to how the woman can change her behavior to minimize the risk of rape, and the various ridiculous, non-lethal weapons she may acceptably carry, such as whistles, keys, mace, or that weapon which really sends shivers down a rapist's spine, the portable cellular phone. . . .

The advice not to resist a criminal assault and simply hand over the goods is founded on the notion that one's life is of incalculable value, and that no amount of property is worth it. Put aside, for a moment, the outrageousness of the suggestion that a criminal who proffers lethal violence should be treated as if he has instituted a new social contract: "I will not hurt or kill you if you give me what I want." For years, feminists have labored to educate people that rape is not about sex, but about domination, degradation, and control. Evidently, someone needs to inform the law enforcement establishment and the media that kidnapping, robbery, carjacking, and assault are not about property. . . .

It is impossible to address the problem of rampant crime without talking about the moral responsibility of the intended victim. Crime is rampant because the law-abiding, each of us, condone it, excuse it, permit it, submit to it. We permit and encourage it because we do not fight back, immediately, then and there, where it happens. Crime is not rampant because we do not have enough prisons, because judges and prosecutors are too soft, because the police are hamstrung with absurd technicalities. The defect is there, in our character. We are a nation of cowards and shirkers. . . .

One who values his life and takes seriously his responsibilities to his family and community will possess and cultivate the means of fighting back, and will retaliate when threatened with death or grievous injury to himself or a loved one. He will never be content to rely solely on others for his safety, or to think he has done all that is possible by being aware of his surroundings and taking measures of avoidance. Let's not mince words: He will be armed, will be trained in the use of his weapon, and will defend himself when faced with lethal violence.

Fortunately, there is a weapon for preserving life and liberty that can be wielded effectively by almost anyone—the handgun. Small and light enough to be carried habitually, lethal, but unlike the knife or sword, not demanding great skill or strength, it truly is the "great equalizer." Requiring only hand-eye coordination and a modicum of ability to remain cool under pressure, it can be used effectively by the old and the weak against the young and the strong, by the one against the many.

The handgun is the only weapon that would give a lone female jogger a chance of prevailing against a gang of thugs intent on rape, a teacher a chance of protecting children at recess from a madman intent on massacring them, a family of tourists waiting at a mid-town subway station the means to protect themselves from a gang of teens armed with razors and knives.

Jeffrey R. Snyder, "A Nation of Cowards," *Public Interest*, Fall 1993.

Document 4: The Economic Costs of Gun Violence

One of the arguments in favor of penalizing the gun industry for violence in which guns are involved is that gun violence costs society a great deal of money for medical care, policing, and prosecution. The statement below briefly summarizes some of the costs associated with gun misuse.

The cost to treat victims of firearm violence is overwhelming. Firearm-related injuries make up 0.5% of all injuries, yet they represent 9% of total cost of injury over a lifetime. Almost 85% of all health-care expenses due to gunshot injuries and fatalities is charged to taxpayers.

Estimates of the total cost of gun violence vary. Researchers Wendy Max and Dorothy P. Rice of the University of California School of Nursing estimate that the 1990 costs of direct medical spending and lost productivity in the United States totaled $20.4 billion. In a study appearing in the Textbook of Penetrating Trauma, researchers concluded that the total 1992 cost of firearm violence was $112 billion when taking into consideration direct medical costs, lost productivity, and lost quality of life. This study also reported that each of the estimated 4.91 billion bullets sold in 1992 represented $23 in costs due to firearm violence, including $0.60 in medical and emergency services, $7.20 in lost productivity, and $15.10 in pain, suffering, and lost quality of life. One news article reported that the average expense of each incidence of gun violence totals well over $300,000.

The financial costs of gun violence place a heavy burden on trauma care centers. Between 1986 and 1991, 92 of the 549 trauma care centers in the United States closed. Because many gunshot victims are uninsured, almost 85% of medical charges due to gunshots are paid by taxpayers through public health care and public debt.

Hospital fees are structured so that insured patients cover the losses due to uninsured patients. This means that private health insurance plans compensate most of the medical costs caused by guns, even though they pay for only one-fourth of the actual injuries. The costs of treating uninsured gunshot victims that aren't picked up through public health care are passed on to those privately insured and paying higher premiums. Moreover, hospitals must charge more for particular procedures in order to compensate for the uninsured. Therefore non-gun owners who are taxpayers and privately insured are paying for the problems created by widespread gun ownership and availability.

Coalition to Stop Gun Violence, "Economic Costs of Gun Violence." www.gunfree.org/csgv/bsc_eco.htm.

Document 5: Prosecuting Criminals Saves Lives

Charlton Heston, an actor and the president of the National Rifle Association, believes it is not right to hold gun manufacturers responsible for gun violence. Individuals are responsible for their own actions, he states in the following excerpt from a speech he gave at Yale University. Heston believes that problems with gun violence can best be solved by enforcing already existing gun laws.

If you drove into Richmond, Virginia, today, you'd be greeted by billboards with giant words that say, "An illegal gun gets you five years in federal prison." These warn all felons that Project Exile is in effect. Project Exile simply enforces existing federal law. Project Exile means every convicted felon caught with a gun, no matter what he's doing, will go to prison for five years. No parole, no early releases, no discussion, period.

My, my—incarcerating armed felons. What a novel idea. It works, like no other anti-crime policy ever proposed. Project Exile, in its first year in

Richmond, cut gun homicides by 62 percent. And as you'd expect, related gun crimes like robbery, rape and assault also plummeted. That means hundreds of people in Richmond today are alive and intact who, without Project Exile, would be dead or bleeding.

For years the NRA has demanded that Project Exile be deployed nationwide. Makes sense, huh? The laws are already on the books. Just enforce them.

But Bill Clinton won't do it. When he says he's serious about fighting crime, consider that as a matter of policy—as a matter of policy—the Clinton Administration is not prosecuting violations of federal gun law. In fact, they reversed the Bush Administration's policy of prosecuting felons with guns. Instead, with plea bargains, a wink and a nod, they've been letting armed felons off the hook. From 1992 to 1998, prosecutions have been cut almost in half.

So while Project Exile was saving lives in Richmond, federal prosecution for gun law violations everywhere else dropped by 46 percent. . . .

Everyone remembers that media love-child, the Brady Bill. Mr. Clinton repeatedly claims that a quarter million handguns have been prevented from falling into the hands of convicted felons. But nobody is reporting what matters to you: How many of those quarter million people were convicted and taken off your streets for the federal crime of being a felon trying to buy a gun? Try nine! . . .

Maybe you think a politician's lies can't hurt you. But let me tell you, armed felons can. Passing laws is what keeps politicians' careers alive. Enforcing laws is what keeps you alive.

Charlton Heston, speech to the Yale University Political Union, April 16, 1999. www.nrahq.org/heston.

Document 6: A Well-Regulated Militia

Legal scholars have been debating the intent of the Second Amendment almost since it was written. The following document excerpts "Commentaries on the Constitution of the United States" by Joseph Story, an early Supreme Court justice. Writing in 1833, Story emphasizes the importance of a citizen militia and the right to bear arms.

The next amendment is: "A well regulated militia being necessary to the security of a free state, the right of the people to keep and bear arms shall not be infringed."

The importance of this article will scarcely be doubted by any persons, who have duly reflected upon the subject. The militia is the natural defense of a free country against sudden foreign invasions, domestic insurrections, and domestic usurpations of power by rulers. It is against sound policy for a free people to keep up large military establishments and standing armies in time of peace, both from the enormous expenses, with which they are attended, and the facile means, which they afford to ambitious and unprincipled rulers, to subvert the government, or trample upon the rights of the people. The right of the citizens to keep and bear arms has justly been considered, as the palladium of the liberties of a republic; since it offers a strong moral check against the usurpation and arbitrary power of rulers; and will generally, even if these are successful in the first instance, enable the people to resist and triumph over them. And yet, though this truth would seem so clear, and the importance of a well regulated militia would seem so undeniable, it cannot be disguised, that among the American people there is a growing indifference to any system of militia discipline, and a strong disposition, from a sense of its burdens, to be rid.

Quoted in Guncite, "The Second Amendment: Quotes from Commentators." www.guncite.com/gc2ndcom.html.

Document 7: *U.S. v. Miller*

The Supreme Court has ruled on only a few cases relating to the Second Amendment. One of those, U.S. v. *Miller is considered a landmark primarily because Supreme Court rulings on gun control are so rare.* Miller *involved two men who claimed that the 1934 National Firearms Act illegally infringed on their right to have a sawed-off shotgun. A lower court had declared the federal law unconstitutional, but the Supreme Court overturned that decision, ruling that sawed-off shotguns were not a likely militia tool and were therefore not protected by the Second Amendment. The Court's ruling is excerpted below.*

In the absence of any evidence tending to show that possession or use of a "shotgun having a barrel of less than eighteen inches in length" at this time has some reasonable relationship to the preservation or efficiency of a well regulated militia, we cannot say that the Second Amendment guarantees the right to keep and bear such an instrument. Certainly it is not within judicial notice that this weapon is any part of the ordinary military equipment or that its use could contribute to the common defense. *Aymette v. State*, 2 Humphreys (Tenn.) 154, 158.

The Constitution as originally adopted granted to the Congress power "to provide for calling forth the militia to execute the laws of the union, suppress insurrections and repel invasions; to provide for organizing, arming, and disciplining, the militia, and for governing such part of them as may be employed in the service of the United States, reserving to the states respectively, the appointment of the officers, and the authority of training the militia according to the discipline prescribed by Congress." With obvious purpose to assure the continuation and render possible the effectiveness of such forces the declaration and guarantee of the Second Amendment were made. It must be interpreted and applied with that end in view.

The militia which the states were expected to maintain and train is set in contrast with troops which they were forbidden to keep without the consent of Congress. The sentiment of the time strongly disfavored standing armies; the common view was that adequate defense of country and laws could be secured through the militia—civilians primarily, soldiers on occasion.

The signification attributed to the term militia appears from the debates in the convention, the history and legislation of colonies and states, and the writings of approved commentators. These show plainly enough that the militia comprised all males physically capable of acting in concert for the common defense. "A body of citizens enrolled for military discipline." And further, that ordinarily when called for service these men were expected to appear bearing arms supplied by themselves and of the kind in common use at the time. . . .

Most if not all of the states have adopted provisions touching the rights to keep and bear arms. Differences in the language employed in these have naturally led to somewhat variant conclusions concerning the scope of the right guaranteed. But none of them seem to afford any material support for the challenged ruling of the court below.

We are unable to accept the conclusion of the court below and the challenged judgment must be reversed.

Justice McReynolds, *U.S. v. Miller*, opinion text. www.cilp.org/Fed-Ct/Supreme/Flite/opinions/307US174.htm.

Document 8: The Brady Act

The Brady Act is the most sweeping federal gun-control measure passed in recent years. To achieve its goal of making it more difficult for criminals to purchase firearms, the act mandates background checks on prospective gun buyers. In the following statement, dated Thursday, February 26, 1998, U.S. deputy attorney general Eric Holder provides a progress report on the Brady Act and the federal background check system.

This Saturday marks the fourth anniversary of President Clinton's Brady Act, which has stopped hundreds of thousands of over-the-counter handgun sales to felons, fugitives and others who are prohibited by the law from getting one.

As you may know, the Brady Act requires that a national instant check system be up and running by the end of this November. It will be. The FBI has developed a computer system that can store and manage the data necessary to perform background checks instantly. And they are loading in a variety of federal records that show who is legally ineligible, such as military dishonorable discharge records.

The Brady Act and federal funding have helped spark a nationwide drive to computerize criminal history records. When the Brady Act became law, fewer than 20 percent of the country's criminal history records were computerized, sharable and complete. Just four years later, that share has doubled. By the end of the year, it should be 50 percent.

This is progress, but this Administration's goal is the most complete criminal history records system possible. The Justice Department has distributed more than $200 million to help states improve their criminal history record systems. We need Congress to keep funding improvements, and we need the states to work as hard as they can to bring their records into shape for the twenty-first century.

Computerized criminal history records don't just stop illegal gun sales —they help states spot job applicants who are barred from positions caring for children, the elderly and the disabled. They also help police determine whether a suspect is the subject of a domestic violence restraining order and help judges determine the appropriate sentences.

The Brady Act has helped keep guns out of the wrong hands. It will keep making a difference—if everyone does what they can to improve criminal history records.

U.S. Department of Justice, "Statement of Deputy Attorney Eric Holder on the Anniversary of the Brady Bill," February 26, 1998.

Document 9: America's Gun Culture

Why are Americans so enamored with guns? Renowned historian Richard Hofstadter suggests that America's gun culture developed not through its Wild West history alone but also through its deeply ingrained distrust of government. Here is an excerpt from an essay Hofstadter wrote on American violence.

It is very easy, in interpreting American history, to give the credit and the blame for almost everything to the frontier, and certainly this temptation is particularly strong where guns are concerned. After all, for the first 250 years of their history Americans were an agricultural people with a continuing history of frontier expansion. At the very beginning the wild continent abounded with edible game, and a colonizing people still struggling to control the wilderness and still living very close to the subsistence level found wild game an important supplement to their diet. Moreover, there were no enforceable feudal inhibitions against poaching by the common man, who was free to roam where he could and shoot what he could and who ate better when he shot better. Furthermore, all farmers, but especially farmers in a lightly settled agricultural country, need guns for the control of wild vermin and predators. The wolf, as we still say, has to be kept from the door.

Finally, and no less imperatively, there were the Indians, who were all too often regarded by American frontiersmen as another breed of wild animal. The situation of the Indians, constantly under new pressures from white encroachments, naturally commands modern sympathy. But they were in fact, partly from the very desperation of their case, often formidable, especially in the early days when they were an all important force in the international rivalries of England, France, and Spain in North America. Like the white man they had guns, and like him they committed massacres. Modern critics of our culture who, like Susan Sontag, seem to know nothing of American history, who regard the white race as a "cancer" and assert that the United States was "founded on a genocide," may fantasize that the Indians fought according to the rules of the Geneva Convention. But in the tragic conflict of which they were to be the chief victims, they were capable of striking terrible blows. In King Philip's War (1675–76) they damaged half the towns of New England, destroyed a dozen, and killed an estimated one out of every sixteen males of military age among the settlers. Later the Deerfield and other frontier massacres left powerful scars on the frontier memory, and in the formative days of the colonial period wariness of sudden Indian raids and semimilitary preparations to combat them were common on the western borders of settlements. Men and women, young and old, were all safer if they could command a rifle. "A well grown boy," remembered the Reverend Joseph Doddridge of his years on the Virginia frontier, "at the age of twelve or thirteen years, was furnished with a small rifle and shot-pouch. He then became a fort soldier, and had his port-hole assigned him. Hunting squirrels, turkeys, and raccoons, soon made him expert in the use of his gun."

That familiarity with the rifle, which was so generally inculcated on the frontier, had a good deal to do with such successes as Americans had in the battles of the Revolution. The Pennsylvania rifle, developed by German immigrants, was far superior to Brown Bess, the regulation military musket used by British troops. This blunt musket, an inaccurate weapon at any considerable distance, was used chiefly to gain the effect of mass firepower in open field maneuvers at relatively close range. The long, slender Pennsylvania rifle, which had a bored barrel that gave the bullet a spin, had a flatter and more direct trajectory, and in skilled hands it became a precision instrument. More quickly loaded and effective at a considerable distance, it was singularly well adapted not only to the shooting of squirrels but to the woodsman's shoot-and-hide warfare. It struck such terror into the hearts of British regulars as to cause George Washington to ask that as many of his troops as possible be dressed in the frontiersman's hunting shirt, since the British thought "every such person a complete Marksman." The rifle went a long way to make up for the military inconsistencies and indifferent discipline of American militiamen, and its successes helped to instill in the American mind a conviction of the complete superiority of the armed yeoman to the military professionals of Europe.

What began as a necessity of agriculture and the frontier took hold as a sport and as an ingredient in the American imagination. Before the days of spectator sports, when competitive athletics became a basic part of popular culture, hunting and fishing probably were the chief American sports, sometimes wantonly pursued, as in the decimation of the bison. But for millions of American boys, learning to shoot and above all graduating from toy guns and receiving the first real rifle of their own were milestones of life, veritable rites of passage that certified their arrival at manhood. (It is still argued by some defenders of our gun culture, and indeed conceded by some of its critics, that the gun cannot and will not be given up because it is a basic symbol of masculinity. But the trouble with all such glib Freudian generalities is that they do not explain cultural variations: they do not tell us why men elsewhere have *not* found the gun essential to their masculinity.)

What was so decisive in the winning of the West and the conquest of the Indian became a standard ingredient in popular entertainment. In the penny-dreadful Western and then in films and on television, the western man, quick on the draw, was soon an acceptable hero of violence. He found his successors in the private eye, the FBI agent, and in the gangster himself, who so often provides a semilegitimate object of hero worship, a man with loyalties, courage, and a code of his own—even in films purporting to show that crime does not pay. All mass cultures have their stereotyped heroes, and none are quite free of violence; but the United States has shown an unusual penchant for the isolated, wholly individualistic detective, sheriff, or villain, and its entertainment portrays the solution of melodramatic conflicts much more commonly than, say, the English, as arising not out of ratiocination or some scheme of moral order but out of ready and ingenious violence. Every Walter Mitty has had his moment when he is Gary Cooper, stalking the streets in *High Noon* with his gun at the ready. D.H. Lawrence may have had something, after all, when he made his characteristically bold, impressionistic, and unflattering judgment that "the essential American soul is hard, isolate, stoic, and a killer." It was the notion cherished also by Hemingway in his long romance with war and hunting and with the other sports that end in death.

However, when the frontier and its ramifications are given their due, they fall far short of explaining the persistence of the American gun culture. Why is the gun still so prevalent in a culture in which only about 4 percent of the country's workers now make their living from farming, a culture that for the last century and a half has had only a tiny fragment of its population actually in contact with a frontier, that, in fact, has not known a true frontier for three generations? Why did the United States alone among industrial societies cling to the idea that a substantially unregulated supply of guns among its city populations is a safe and acceptable thing? This is, after all, not the only nation with a frontier history.

One factor that could not be left out of any adequate explanation of the tenacity of our gun culture is the existence of an early American political creed that has had a surprisingly long life, albeit much of it now is in an underground popular form. It has to do with the anti-militaristic traditions of radical English Whiggery, which were taken over and intensified in colonial America, especially during the generation preceding the American Revolution, and which became an integral part of the American political tradition. The popular possession of the gun was a central point in a political doctrine that became all but sacrosanct in the Revolution: a doctrine that rested upon faith in the civic virtue and military prowess of the yeoman; belief in the degeneration of England and in the sharp decline of "the liberties of Englishmen" on their original home soil; and a great fear of a standing army as one of the key dangers to this body of ancient liberties. The American answer to civic and military decadence was the armed yeoman.

Richard Hofstadter and Michael Wallace, eds., *American Violence: A Documentary History.* New York: Knopf, 1970.

Document 10: The Militia Movement

Many Americans firmly believe that the Second Amendment unequivocally protects an individual's right to own firearms. This is a view often expressed by supporters of the militia movement, who believe that the federal gun-control measures violate the Constitution and that Americans have a duty to resist them. These excerpts from an article in the September 1994 issue of Guns and Ammo *express this sentiment.*

A ban of so called assault rifles today will become a ban on your Remington 1100 tomorrow—bet on it. . . . The avowed goal of those in our very government is to strip us of our rights under the Second Amendment. . . .

The Second Amendment is a part of this Constitution and is not in the authority of Congress to alter save by an amending process as submitted to the states. No 51–49 vote can legally supersede it. . . . Congress would be breaking the supreme law if it infringed on our Second Amendment rights. . . . I'm not in the habit of handing over my guns to any criminal, regardless of title or elected office. . . .

We cannot hope to prevail against a tyrannical government armed with fully automatic weapons when we are reduced to bolt actions or worse. . . . You see, it is not street crime driving the anti-gunners, it is the complete disarmament of the American populace. If they've taken our semi's, they'll eventually get the rest without risk. Do I know what I'm suggesting here? Yes, I do.

I am speaking of the specter of civil war while adamantly hoping it can be avoided.

Stephen Weaver, "Freedom's Last Stand: Are You Willing to Fight for Your Guns?" *Guns and Ammo,* September 1994.

ORGANIZATIONS TO CONTACT

The editors have compiled the following list of organizations concerned with the issues debated in this book. The descriptions are derived from materials provided by the organizations. All have publications or information available for interested readers. The list was compiled on the date of publication of the present volume; the information provided here may change. Be aware that many organizations take several weeks or longer to respond to inquiries, so allow as much time as possible.

Bureau of Alcohol, Tobacco, and Firearms (ATF)
Office of Liaison and Public Information
650 Massachusetts Ave. NW, Room 8290
Washington, DC 20226
(202) 927-8500 • fax: (202) 927-8868
e-mail: fea@atfhq.atf.treas.gov • website: http://www.atf.treas.gov

The ATF, part of the U.S. Department of the Treasury, is charged with reducing violent crime, collecting revenue, and protecting the public. The bureau enforces federal regulations relating to alcohol, tobacco, firearms, explosives, and arson. It also publishes quarterly bulletins, newsletters, and a number of other publications, including *Gun Shows: Brady Checks and Crime Gun Traces*.

Citizens Committee for the Right to Keep and Bear Arms (CCRKBA)
12500 NE Tenth Pl.
Bellevue, WA 98005
(425) 454-4911 • fax: (425) 451-3959
e-mail: info@ccrkba.org • website: http://www.ccrkba.org

The committee believes that the U.S. Constitution's Second Amendment guarantees and protects the right of individual Americans to own guns. It works to educate the public concerning this right and to lobby legislators to prevent the passage of gun-control laws. The committee is affiliated with the Second Amendment Foundation. It distributes the books *Gun Laws of America, Gun Rights Fact Book, Origin of the Second Amendment*, and *Point Blank: Guns and Violence in America*.

Coalition to Stop Gun Violence

1000 16th St. NW, Ste. 603
Washington, DC 10036
(202) 530-0340 • fax: (202) 530-0331
e-mail: noguns@aol.com • website: http://www.gunfree.org

The Coalition to Stop Gun Violence is comprised of forty-four national organizations and 100,000 members working to reduce gun violence. The coalition works toward its goal by fostering effective community and national action. Its publications include various informational sheets on gun violence, the *Stop Gun Violence Newsletter*, and the *Firearms Litigation Reporter.*

Gun Owners Action League (GOAL)

37 Pierce St.
P.O. Box 567
Northboro, MA 01532
(508) 393-5333 • fax: (508) 393-5222
e-mail: staff@goal.org • website: http://www.goal.org

GOAL is the official state firearms organization of Massachusetts. Through its website, it provides information, speakers, and educational materials to the general public. GOAL also lobbies for government action favoring gun owners' rights and offers gun safety programs. GOAL publishes a newsletter, the *Message*, as well as law updates.

Gun Owners of America (GOA)
Gun Owners Foundation (GOF)

8001 Forbes Pl., Ste. 102
Springfield, VA 22151
(703) 321-8585 • fax: (703) 321-8408
e-mail: goamail@gunowners.org • gofmail@gunowners.org
website: http://www.gunowners.org

GOA is a lobbying organization that actively encourages political action from its 200,000 members. It publishes a newsletter, fact sheets, and legislative and other information. GOF is the educational and legal arm of Gun Owners of America. It provides legal assistance for law-abiding gun owners and produces educational books and videos on Second Amendment topics.

Handgun Control, Inc.
1225 Eye St. NW, Ste. 1100
Washington, DC 20005
(202) 898-0792 • fax: (202) 371-9615
website: http://www.handguncontrol.org
A citizen lobby working for the federal regulation of the manufacture, sale, and civilian possession of handguns and automatic weapons, the organization successfully promoted the passage of the Brady law, which mandated a five-day waiting period for the purchase of handguns. The lobby publishes the quarterly newsletter *Progress Report* and the book *Guns Don't Die—People Do*, as well as legislative reports and pamphlets.

Independence Institute
14142 Denver West Pkwy., Ste. 185
Golden, CO 80401
(303) 279-6536 • fax: (303) 279-4176
e-mail: webmngr@i2i.org • website: http://www.i2i.org
The Independence Institute is a pro–free market think tank that supports gun ownership as a civil liberty and a constitutional right. Its publications include books and booklets opposing gun control, such as *Children and Guns: Sensible Solutions, The Assault Weapon Panic: "Political Correctness" Takes Aim at the Constitution*, and *The Samurai, the Mountie, and the Cowboy.*

The Lion & Lamb Project
4300 Montgomery Ave., Ste. 104
Bethesda, MD 20814
(301) 654-3091 • fax: (301) 718-8192
e-mail: lionlamb@lionlamb.org • website: http://www.lionlamb.org
The Lion & Lamb Project is a national grassroots initiative providing information about the effects of violent entertainment, toys, and games on children's behavior. It offers workshops and educational materials and sponsors events such as violent toy trade-ins. It publishes a Parent Action Kit focusing on how violence is a learned behavior and what parents can do about it, and *Toys for Peace*, a manual for organizing toy trade-ins.

National Center for Policy Analysis (NCPA)
12655 N. Central Expy., Ste. 720
Dallas, TX 75243-1739
(972) 386-6272 • fax: (972) 386-0924
e-mail: ncpa@public-policy.org • website: http://www.ncpa.org

The NCPA's primary goal is to develop and promote private alternatives to government regulation and control and to encourage reliance on the strengths of the competitive, entrepreneurial sector. It provides analysis of and information about a variety of policy issues, including taxation, health care, social security, the environment, and criminal justice. NCPA publishes "Off Target with Gun Controls," "Suing Gun Manufacturers: Hazardous to Our Health," "Myths About Gun Control," and other publications.

National Crime Prevention Council (NCPC)
1700 K St. NW, 2nd Fl.
Washington, DC 20006-3817
(202) 261-4111 • fax: (202) 296-1356
e-mail: webmaster@ncpc.org • website: http://www.ncpc.org

The NCPC is a branch of the U.S. Department of Justice. It works to teach Americans how to reduce crime and addresses the causes of crime in its programs and educational materials. It provides readers with information on gun control and gun violence. The NCPC's publications include the newsletter *Catalyst,* which is published ten times a year, the book *Reducing Gun Violence: What Communities Can Do,* and the booklet "Making Children, Families, and Communities Safer from Violence."

National Institute of Justice (NIJ)
National Criminal Justice Reference Service (NCJRS)
Box 6000
Rockville, MD 20849
(301) 519-5500 • (800) 851-3420
e-mail: askncjrs@ncjrs.org • website: http://www.ncjrs.org

A component of the Office of Justice Programs of the U.S. Department of Justice, the NIJ supports research on crime, criminal behavior, and crime prevention. It has a library of criminal justice literature that can be borrowed through local libraries. The National Criminal Justice Reference Service acts as a clearinghouse that provides information and research about criminal justice. Its publications include the research briefs "Reducing Youth Gun Violence: An Overview of Programs and Initiatives," "Impacts of the 1994 Assault Weapons Ban," and "Homicide in Eight U.S. Cities: Trends, Context, and Policy Implications."

National Rifle Association of America (NRA)
11250 Waples Mill Rd.
Fairfax, VA 22030
(703) 267-1000 • fax: (703) 267-3989
website: http://www.nra.org

The NRA is America's largest organization of gun owners. It is the primary lobbying group for those who oppose gun-control laws. The NRA believes that such laws violate the U.S. Constitution and do nothing to reduce crime. In addition to its monthly magazines *American Rifleman, American Hunter,* and *Incites,* the NRA publishes numerous books, bibliographies, reports, and pamphlets on gun ownership, gun safety, and gun control.

Second Amendment Foundation (SAF)
12500 NE Tenth Pl.
Bellevue, WA 98005
(425) 454-7012 • (800) 426-4302 • fax: (425) 451-3959
e-mail: info@saf.org • website: http://www.saf.org

The foundation defends citizens' rights to privately own and possess firearms. It believes many gun-control laws violate this right. SAF maintains biographical archives and a library, copies statistics, and publishes *Journal on Firearms and Public Policy, Gun Week, Gun News Digest, Second Amendment Reporter, Women and Guns,* and other monographs and pamphlets.

Violence Policy Center (VPC)
1140 19th St. NW, Ste. 600
Washington, DC 20036
e-mail: comment@vpc.org • website: http://www.vpc.org

The center is an educational foundation that conducts research on firearms violence. It supports gun-control measures and works to educate the public concerning the dangers of guns. The center's publications include the report "Cease Fire: A Comprehensive Strategy to Reduce Firearms Violence" and the books *NRA: Money, Firepower, and Fear* and *Assault Weapons and Accessories in America.*

FOR FURTHER READING

Books

Geoffrey Canada, *Fist Stick Knife Gun: A Personal History of Violence in America*. Boston: Beacon, 1995. The author's personal account of growing up in a violent neighborhood of the South Bronx, New York, allows him to examine the roots of violence in America's children.

Gregg Lee Carter, *The Gun Control Movement*. New York: Twayne, 1997. Sociological overview of the history of the gun-control movement as a social movement, American attitudes toward guns and gun control, and the Second Amendment.

Edward F. Dolan and Margaret M. Scariano, *Guns in the United States*. New York: Franklin Watts, 1994. A young people's history of guns in America and the issues surrounding gun violence.

Freya Ottem Hanson, *The Second Amendment: The Right to Own Guns*. Springfield, NJ: Enslow, 1999. Young people's history of the Second Amendment and brief overview of the gun-control debate today.

Gary Kleck and Don B. Kates, *The Great American Gun Debate*. San Francisco: Pacific Research Institute for Public Policy, 1997. Collection of research-based essays by the authors and two others. The authors attempt to "sort out the facts," paying particular attention to what they view as the demonization of guns. Topics include media bias, guns and self-defense, constitutional issues, and the flaws in some of the arguments for gun control.

Erik Larson, *Lethal Passage: How the Travels of a Single Handgun Expose the Roots of America's Gun Crisis*. New York: Crown, 1994. Starting with a school shooting, Larson investigates the source of the gun involved. This leads him to an examination of many aspects of guns in America—from manufacturers to dealers to shooters to laws and law enforcement. He concludes that gun-control laws must be made stricter and be enforced more effectively.

Lee Nisbit, ed., *The Gun Control Debate: You Decide*. Buffalo, NY: Prometheus, 1990. Twenty-four essays examining Americans' views of guns, guns and crime, guns for self-defense, and the Second Amendment.

Tamara L. Roleff, ed., *Gun Control: Opposing Viewpoints*. San Diego: Greenhaven Press, Inc., 1997. Two dozen articles from various sources present viewpoints on several aspects of the gun-control debate: guns as a hazard, the Second Amendment, guns and self-defense, and gun violence.

William Weir, *A Well-Regulated Militia*. North Haven, CT: Archon Books, 1997. The author joined both Handgun Control, Inc., and the National Rifle Association—two opposing groups in the debate on gun control—as part of his research on the gun-control debate. The author finds problems with both organizations' perspectives as he examines the Second Amendment, guns and crime, and gun control. Weir suggests that, more than gun control, America needs to address the social issues that lead to crime and violence.

Periodicals

Jerry Adler and Karen Springen, "How to Fight Back," *Newsweek*, May 3, 1999.

American Rifleman, "The Armed Citizen," May 1999.

———, "Hired Guns Take Aim at Your Guns," May 1999.

Pam Belluck, "Weary of Gun Violence, Chicago Considers Suit," *New York Times*, June 12, 1998.

Frank Bruni, "Senate Wrangles over Gun Control, Youth Violence," *New York Times*, May 12, 1999.

Fox Butterfield, "New Data Point Blame at Gun Makers," *New York Times*, November 28, 1998.

———, "Study Exposes Illegal Traffic in New Guns," *New York Times*, February 21, 1999.

Osha Gray Davidson, "Guns for All Ages," *New York Times*, March 21, 1998.

David Firestone, "Georgia Bill Aims to Block Anti-Gun Lawsuits," *New York Times*, February 9, 1999.

Tom Hays, "Fifteen of Twenty-Five Gun Makers Found Liable in N.Y. Shootings," *St. Paul Pioneer Press*, January 15, 1999.

Michael Janofsky, "Fighting Crime by Making Federal Case About Guns," *New York Times*, February 10, 1999.

Tamar Lewin, "Bloodshed in a Schoolyard," *New York Times*, March 26, 1998.

John R. Lott Jr., "Will More Guns Mean Less Crime?" *Consumer's Research*, December 1998.

Barry Meier, "Guns Don't Kill; Gun Makers Do?" *New York Times*, April 16, 1995.

Mike Mitka, "Medical Groups Say Physicians Can Help Keep Kids from Killing," *JAMA*, June 17, 1998.

Lance Morrow, "Coming to Clarity About Guns," *Newsweek*, May 3, 1999.

Newsweek, "Moving Beyond the Blame Game," May 17, 1999.

New York Times, "Guns and Responsibility," March 27, 1998.

———, "Suit Allowed Against Gun Maker for Killings," April 12, 1995.

Gustav Niebuhr, "Presbyterians Urged to Keep Handguns Out of the Home," *New York Times*, June 20, 1998.

Kathleen M. Sullivan, "Why the Brady Law Is Unconstitutional," *New York Times*, December 6, 1996.

Internet Sources

American Bar Association, Coordinating Committee on Gun Violence, "Facts About Gun Violence and ABA Resolution," July 28, 1998. www.abanet.org.

American Civil Liberties Union, "Gun Control," 1996. www.aclu.org/library/aaguns.html.

American Derringer Corporation, "Children and Firearms Safety," 1997. www.amderringer.com/kidsafety.html.bsc_eco.htm.

J.T. Brady, "'Smart' Guns on the Way," November 17, 1998. www.apbonline.com/safestreets/1998/11/17/smartguns_01.html.

Center for the Study and Prevention of Violence, "CSPV Fact Sheet." www.colorado.edu/cspv.

Coalition to Stop Gun Violence, "Economic Costs of Gun Violence." www.gunfree.org/csgv/bsc_eco.htm.

———, "The Facts." www.gunfree.org/csgv/basicinfo.htm.

———, "Guns in Schools." www.gunfree.org/csgv/bsc_sch.htm.

———, "A Partial Summary of Federal Regulations Applicable to Firearms and Ammunition." www.gunfree.org/csgv/fedregs.htm.

———, "Unintentional Shootings." www.gunfree.org/csgv/bsc_uni.htm.

Brian Doherty, "Does Gun Control Discriminate Against the Poor?" *Reason Online*. www.reasonmag.com/bi/guns.html.

Guncite, "International Violent Death Rates," June 25, 1999. www.guncite.com/gcgvintl.html.

————, "The Second Amendment: Quotes from Commentators." www.guncite.com/gc2ndcom.html.

Gun Owners Foundation, "Firearms Fact-Sheet," February 1997. www.gunowners.org/fstb.htm.

GunTruths.Com, "Proof Positive: Gun Control Increases Violent Crime—the Latest Data from Australia." www.guntruths.com.

Handgun Control, Inc., "Carrying Concealed Weapons: Questions and Answers." www.handguncontrol.org.

————, "The Gun Industry: Creating a Market Ignoring Safety." www.handguncontrol.org.

Hearst Newspapers, "Guns in America" (three-part series), 1997. www.chron.com/content/chronicle/nation/guns.

Charlton Heston, "Closing Remarks to Members," NRA Annual Meeting, May 1, 1999. www.nrahq.org/heston.

————, speech to the Yale University Political Union, April 16, 1999. www.nrahq.org/heston.

Join Together Online, "Gun Owners and General Public Want Stronger Gun Laws." www.jointogether.org.

————, "Why Gun Control Remains Elusive," May 9, 1999. www.jointogether.org.

Justice McReynolds, *U.S. v. Miller* opinion text. www.cilp.org/Fed Ct/Supreme/Flite/opinions/307US174.htm.

David Schiller, "Project Exile," 1998. www.vahv.org/Exile/.

Second Amendment Foundation, "Women Would Break Gun Carry Ban When Necessary." www.saf.org.

Helen Smith, "It's Not the Guns," Nando Media, May 1999. www.nandotimes.com.

Ed Stone, "Gun Control: Enough Already!" www.lafn.org/education/swl/clgc1.htm.

Student Pledge Against Gun Violence, "I Pledge." www.pledge.org/pledge.html.

Jacob Sullum, "Nuisance Suits," *Reason Online*, November 18, 1998.

www.reasonmag.com/sullum/111898.html.

Robert W. Tracinski, "An Unjust Assault on Guns," Ayn Rand Institute. www.aynrand.org/medialink/guns.shtml

J.D. Tuccille, "High Noon in the Courtroom," January 24, 1999. http://civilliberty.about.com.

U.S. Department of Justice, "The President's Anti-Gang and Youth Violence Strategy: Success Stories," 1997. www.usdoj.gov/ag/success.htm.

Violence Policy Center, "Who Dies? A Look at Firearms Death and Injury in America—Revised Edition, Appendix Four: The Second Amendment—No Right to Keep and Bear Arms," February 1999. www.vpc.org/studies/whocont.htm

Oleg Volk, "Guns as Fine Art." www.ddb.com/olegv/guns/fineart.html.

Daphne White, "Why I Started the Lion & Lamb Project." www.lionlamb.org.

James Wright, "Statement Before the Subcommittee on Crime: Ten Irrefutable Facts About Guns," March 31, 1995. http://ns.netacres.com/myers/wright.html.

Websites

Guncite (www.guncite.com). Seeks to protect Second Amendment rights. Contains a wide range of information, articles, and statistics on gun-related topics.

Join Together Online (www.jointogether.org). Contains many news articles related to gun control; favors strict control.

National Center for Policy Analysis (www.ncpa.org). The center is against strong gun control and offers a wide range of articles on the subject.

WORKS CONSULTED

Books

Neal Bernards, *Gun Control.* San Diego: Lucent Books, 1991. Easy-to-read overview of the history of gun control and some of the issues involved. Includes historical photos and illustrations.

Marjolijn Bijlefeld, ed., *The Gun Control Debate: A Documentary History.* Westport, CT: Greenwood, 1997. Anthology containing many very brief excerpts from an array of documents from colonial times to 1996, most from the twentieth century. Connecting material is extremely thin.

John M. Bruce and Clyde Wilcox, eds., *The Changing Politics of Gun Control.* Blue Ridge Summit, PA: Rowman and Littlefield, 1998. Scholarly essays examine a variety of issues, including gun lobbies, evolving weapons technology, the Brady Act, and the Second Amendment.

Tom Diaz, *Making a Killing: The Business of Guns in America.* New York: New Press, 1999. The author views guns as a public health hazard and suggests that they should be dealt with in much the same way the country has dealt with cigarette makers: through laws relating to their "side effects" and lawsuits against the industry.

James Garbarino, *Lost Boys: Why Our Sons Turn Violent and How We Can Save Them.* New York: Balantine Books, 1999. Examines the growing problem of youth violence and offers parents ways to keep this from happening to their children.

Richard Hofstadter and Michael Wallace, eds., *American Violence: A Documentary History.* New York: Knopf, 1970. Collection of historical writings about violent episodes in American history, with brief commentary by the editors and a lengthy introduction by Hofstadter. Ranges from "Pilgrims versus Puritans, 1634" to the 1968 assassination of Robert F. Kennedy. Taken from newspaper, broadcast, eyewitness, and other accounts.

Pam Houston, ed., *Women on Hunting.* Hopewell, NJ: Ecco, 1995. Fiction, nonfiction, and poetry about hunting, written by women.

Mike Huckabee with George Grant, *Kids Who Kill: Confronting Our Culture of Violence.* Nashville: Broadman & Holman, 1998. Examines the growing phenomenon of young killers and suggests that solutions lie in religion and social reform.

William H. Hull, *Up North: Memorable Experiences of Great Deer Hunting.* Edina, MN: self-published. 1996. About four dozen reminiscences by the author and others of deer hunting experiences.

Michael D. Kelleher, *When Good Kids Kill.* Westport, CT: Praeger, 1998. The author examines numerous recent cases of young people with no history of violence who committed murder. He draws conclusions about warning signs and patterns of experience that may be able to help prevent other juvenile homicides.

Jonathan Kellerman, *Savage Spawn: Reflections on Violent Children.* New York: Ballantine, 1999. An extended essay by a novelist and child psychologist examining the reasons for youth violence, with special focus on the psychopathic child. Suggests possible remedies.

Don Kindlon and Michael Thompson, *Raising Cain: Protecting the Emotional Life of Boys.* New York: Ballantine, 1999. Two child psychologists examine the way boys are raised and suggest that the definition of manhood has been made far too narrow. Boys are the victims of a "tyranny of toughness" and need to become more "emotionally literate" in order to become successful, healthy adults.

Gary Kleck, *Point Blank: Guns and Violence in America.* Hawthorne, NY: Aldine de Gruyter, 1991. Scholarly work based on thorough research. The author concludes that guns are successful means of self-defense and crime control.

John R. Lott Jr., *More Guns, Less Crime: Understanding Crime and Gun Control Laws.* Chicago: University of Chicago Press, 1998. Controversial study of guns and crime that finds that more guns in the hands of private citizens means a reduction in crime. Likewise, the study found that states with stronger gun-control measures actually have higher crime and violence rates than those with more permissive gun laws.

Debra Niehoff, *The Biology of Violence: How Understanding the Brain, Behavior, and Environment Can Break the Vicious Circle of Aggression.* New York: Free Press, 1999. Examination of the latest research relating to aggression and violence. New studies of the brain, biochemistry, and other elements lead to the conclusion that violence is to some degree biologically determined. By understanding these things, the author says, we may be able to learn how to end—or at least substantially reduce—society's violence.

Michael Obsatz, *Raising Nonviolent Children in a Violent World.* Minneapolis: Augsburg, 1998. Guidance for parents who are raising children in a culture suffused with violence and violent imagery.

Mark Seltzer, *Serial Killers: Death and Life in America's Wound Culture*. New York: Routledge, 1998. Serial killers did not come into being until the twentieth century. The author examines the lives and acts of several well-known serial killers in the context of what he calls "America's wound culture"—a society whose popular culture and people are beset with a fascination for the macabre.

Periodicals

Associated Press, "Clinton Wants More Money to Trace Guns to Their Source," *St. Paul Pioneer Press*, February 22, 1999.

———, "Forty-Three Percent of American Homes with Kids Have Guns Present, Survey Reveals," *St. Paul Pioneer Press*, November 14, 1998.

———, "Reno: More to Teen Angst than Guns," *St. Paul Pioneer Press*, May 17, 1999.

Paul M. Barrett, "Aiming High: A Lawyer Goes After Gun Manufacturers; Has She Got a Shot?" *Wall Street Journal*, September 17, 1998.

Tad Bartimus, "There Are No Miracle Cures for the Growing Sickness of Violence," *St. Paul Pioneer Press*, May 11, 1999.

Sharon Begley et al., "Why the Young Kill," *Newsweek*, May 3, 1999.

Laura Billings, "What Everyone Sees—Except in the U.S.," *St. Paul Pioneer Press*, May 5, 1999.

James Bovard, "Disarming Those Who Need Guns Most," *Wall Street Journal*, December 23, 1996.

———, "Gun Control's Crippling Misfire," *Washington Times*, January 21, 1997.

John M. Broder, "Supreme Court Rejects Federal School Gun Ban," *Los Angeles Times*, April 27, 1995.

Ronald Brownstein, "Bullets and Ballots," Los Angeles Times-Washington Post News Service, June 21, 1999.

David Brunet, "One Nearly Fatal Hunting Accident Brought Home the Danger of Guns," *St. Paul Pioneer Press*, August 16, 1998.

Stephen Chapman, "Putting Guns in Defensive Hands," *Washington Times*, January 29, 1995.

Richard Cohen, "Armed Nation Bears Deadly Fruit," *San Diego Union-Tribune*, February 23, 1995.

Tom Diaz, "Target: Guns: Opinion," *St. Paul Pioneer Press*, February 18, 1999.

Dianne Feinstein, "Protecting Children from Danger of Guns," *San Diego Union-Tribune*, August 29, 1997.

Samuel Francis, "Finding Safety in Gun Ownership," *Washington Times*, March 10, 1995.

Donna Harrington-Loeuker, "Blown Away," *American School Board Journal*, May 1992.

Bob Herbert, "The 'Elegant' Handgun," *New York Times*, December 4, 1994.

David Hess, "House Defeats Gun Control Bill," *St. Paul Pioneer Press*, June 19, 1999.

———, "House Juvenile Justice Bill May Sink Under Own Weight," *St. Paul Pioneer Press*, June 12, 1999.

Denis Horgan, "Forget Haphazard, Halfhearted Gun 'Control' and Dump Second Amendment Outright," *St. Paul Pioneer Press*, May 21, 1999.

Human Events, "Chicago Professor Discovers More Guns Means Less Crime," June 19, 1998.

Willie Johnson, "Development of Healthy Self-Esteem Might Head Off Future Littletons," *St. Paul Pioneer Press*, May 21, 1999.

Caitlin Kelly, "Gun Control," *Wall Street Journal*, September 12, 1997.

Otto Kreisher, "Gun Ban Could Wind Up Disarming U.S. Troops," *San Diego Union-Tribune*, October 1, 1997.

Charles Laszewski, "Council Member Seeks Lawsuit Against Gun Makers," *St. Paul Pioneer Press*, February 26, 1999.

Jack Lenning, letter, *St. Paul Pioneer Press*, March 4, 1999.

Sanford Levinson, "The Embarrassing Second Amendment," *Yale Law Journal*, vol. 99.

Los Angeles Times, "Lessons of Gun Violence: A Need for Tough Controls," March 10, 1997.

John R. Lott Jr., "Keep Guns out of Lawyers' Hands," *Wall Street Journal*, June 23, 1998.

Alexander MacLeod, "Britain Set to Outlaw Handguns," *Christian Science Monitor*, October 17, 1996.

Robert Stacy McCain, "Concealed Weapons Stop Crime," *Insight*, September 21, 1998.

Mary McGrory, "Guns Are Why," *Washington Post*, April 25, 1999.

R.H. Melton, "Richmond Gun Project Praised," *Washington Post*, June 18, 1998.

Mike Mitka, "Guns as a Public Health Issue," *American Medical News*, February 9, 1998.

E.J. Montini, "V-Chip Can't Match a Full Clip," *North County Times*, March 27, 1998.

Richard Morin, "Aiming for Tighter Control of Guns," *Washington Post National Weekly Edition*, March 31, 1997.

New American, "Antidote for Oppression," March 30, 1998.

Kathleen Parker, "Keep Thought Police Out of Class," *North County Times*, July 11, 1998.

Neal R. Pierce, "Wall of Shame," *St. Paul Pioneer Press*, November 24, 1998.

James Pilcher, "NRA Aims to Head Off Anti-Firearm Litigation," *St. Paul Pioneer Press*, February 5, 1999.

Lucy Quinlivan, "Tougher Gun Laws Go into Effect," *St. Paul Pioneer Press*, January 2, 1999.

Kristin Rand, "Don't Let Firearms Industry Off the Hook," *Christian Science Monitor*, April 18, 1997.

William Raspberry, "Answers That Satisfy Only Ourselves," *Washington Post*, April 3, 1998.

Ruben Rosario, "Economist Analyzes Gun Laws, Sets Off Debate," *St. Paul Pioneer Press*, August 10, 1998.

———, "In Gun Debate, Sorting Out Views a Challenge," *St. Paul Pioneer Press*, August 3, 1999.

———, "Public Health Expert Says Guns Should Be Altered to Prevent Injuries, Death," *St. Paul Pioneer Press*, August 17, 1998.

Michael Ryan, "They're Turning In Their Guns," *Parade*, May 3, 1998.

Christopher Scanlan, "It's 10 PM; Do You Know Where Your Guns Are?" *Christian Science Monitor*, February 10, 1995.

Dave Shiflett, "Have Gun, Will Eat Out," *Wall Street Journal*, February 28, 1995.

Leslie Marmon Silko, "In the Combat Safety Zone," *Hungry Mind Review*, September 1, 1995.

Rachel E. Stassen-Berger, "Father Is Charged After Son Fires Gun," *St. Paul Pioneer Press*, May 20, 1999.

———, "Minneapolis May Take Aim at Gun Industry in Liability Suit," *St. Paul Pioneer Press*, February 19, 1999.

Jacob Sullum, "More Guns, Less Gun Control Might Help Deter Crime," *St. Paul Pioneer Press*, August 11, 1998.

———, "Violent Recreation Nothing New," *St. Paul Pioneer Press*, May 21, 1999.

Robert Suro, "Industry Questioning NRA Role," *Washington Post*, April 25, 1999.

Carol Tavris, "Violence Is a Symptom, Not an Inevitability," *Los Angeles Times*, March 24, 1998.

D.J. Tice, "Linehan Case Typifies Scary Impulse Courts Recently Indulging: Ignoring Law," *St. Paul Pioneer Press*, June 2, 1999.

———, "Target: Guns: Opinion," *St. Paul Pioneer Press*, February 18, 1999.

Brian Toogood, "Some Dangers Unavoidable, but One Emphatically Isn't," *St. Paul Pioneer Press*, June 6, 1999.

Lionel Van Deerlin, "Here's a Move Toward Some Real Gun Control," *San Diego Union-Tribune*, June 25, 1997.

David E. Vandercoy, "The History of the Second Amendment," *Valparaiso Law Review*, 1994.

Sam Walker, "Gun Case May Trigger More Product Suits," *Christian Science Monitor*, May 17, 1995.

Edward Walsh, "GOP Faults Enforcement of Gun Laws," *Washington Post*, May 28, 1999.

Wayne Wangstad, "Shooting Underscores Dangers of Gun-Kid Mix," *St. Paul Pioneer Press*, April 9, 1999.

Washington Times, "Trained Gun Owners More Likely to Keep Firearms Loaded at Home," January 4, 1995.

Mason Weaver, "More Guns Mean Safer Streets," *North County Times*, August 29, 1997.

Robert J. Wooley, "Concealed-Carry Gun Laws Reduce Public Shootings," *St. Paul Pioneer Press*, April 27, 1999.

Thomas Zolper and Seamus McGraw, "Gun Lobby, Child Groups Lock Horns," *Bergen Record*, February 19, 1999.

Pamphlets and Other Materials

Jeff Bingaman, "Bingaman Brings New Juvenile Crime Effort to Greater Albuquerque" (press release), June 30, 1998.

Centers for Disease Control and Prevention, "Facts About Violence Among Youth and Violence in Schools," May 21, 1998.

Citizens Committee for the Right to Keep and Bear Arms, *The Failure of Gun Control, A Task Force Report to the President of the United States, the U.S. Congress, and the American People, Executive Summary*. Bellevue, WA: Citizens Committee for the Right to Keep and Bear Arms, 1989. Provides documentation showing that state gun-control measures have resulted in increased crime rates.

Bill Clinton, remarks to gun-control advocates at a White House conference following the Littleton, Colorado, school massacre. Washington, DC: Office of the White House, May 27, 1999.

———, remarks on gun-control legislation. Washington, DC: Office of the White House, April 27, 1999.

———, remarks on gun-control legislation. Washington, DC: Office of the White House, June 15, 1999.

Hillary Clinton, remarks on gun-control legislation. Washington, DC: Office of the White House, April 27, 1999.

Scott H. Decker, Susan Pennell, and Ami Caldwell, "Illegal Firearms: Access and Use by Arrestees." Washington, DC: National Institute of Justice Research Brief, January 1997.

Departments of Education and Justice, *Early Warning, Timely Response: A Guide to Safe Schools*. Washington, DC: U.S. Department of Education and Department of Justice, 1998.

National Public Radio, *All Things Considered*, July 1, 1999, segment on El Sereno Middle School program to buy back guns.

———, "Gun Control Series," *Morning Edition*, June 14–18, 1999.

Daniel D. Polsby and Dennis Brennan, "Taking Aim at Gun Control," Heartland Institute Policy Study, no. 69, October 30, 1995.

Kristin Rand, "No Right to Keep and Bear Arms." Washington, DC: Violence Policy Center, 1992.

David Sheppard, "Strategies to Reduce Gun Violence" (fact sheet). Washington, DC: U.S. Department of Justice, February 1999. Overview of new government publication *Promising Strategies to Reduce Gun Violence*, which describes sixty promising or innovative strategies implemented by cities around the nation.

Tom W. Smith, "1998 National Gun Policy Survey of the National Opinion Research Center: Research Findings." Chicago: National Opinion Research Center, University of Chicago, May 1999.

William R. Tonso, *Gun Control: White Man's Law*. Bellevue, WA: Second Amendment Foundation, 1997. Contends that gun-control laws are aimed at keeping minorities powerless.

U.S. Department of Justice, *Community Action: Taking Steps to Reduce Youth Gun Violence: Program Summary*. Washington, DC: U.S. Department of Justice, Office of Juvenile Justice and Delinquency Prevention, October 1996. Description of eleven promising programs and information about how to start one in your community.

Violence Policy Center, *Joe Camel with Feathers: How the NRA with Gun and Tobacco Industry Dollars Uses Its Eddie Eagle Program to Market Guns to Kids*. Washington, DC: Violence Policy Center, 1997. Examination of the gun industry's tactics in marketing guns to families and young people.

———, *Young Guns: How the Gun Lobby Nurtures America's Youth Gun Culture*. Washington, DC: Violence Policy Center, 1998. Reproductions of gun advertising and articles that explicitly and implicitly illustrate the gun industry's efforts to recruit youngsters to gun ownership. Includes statistics on young people and firearms-related deaths.

Ken Warner, *Gun Digest, 1998*. Iola, WI: DBI Books/Krause Publications, 1997. Primarily a catalog of guns of all types, accessories, and trade directory. Also contains several articles.

Marianne W. Zawitz, "Guns Used in Crime." Washington, DC: Bureau of Justice Statistics Selected Findings, July 1995. Shows types and sources of guns used in homicides and other crimes.

INDEX

accidents, 24
advertisements, 68, 71–72
American Rifleman
  (magazine), 77, 83
American Shooting Sports
  Council, 77
ammunition, 14, 58
Anderson, Gary, 71–72
assassinations, 13
assault guns, 16, 57
Atlanta, Georgia, 74

background checks, 56
Barnes, Elisa, 68–70
barrel guards, 58
Bash, Bob
  on gun education, 83–84
  on hunting, 81
Billings, Laura, 92–93
Borinsky, Mark, 18–19
Brady, James, 16
Brady, Sarah, 16, 19
Brady Handgun Violence
  Protection Act, 16, 56
Brennan, Dennis, 28
Brown, Richard Maxwell, 85
bullets, 14, 58
Bureau of Alcohol, Tobacco,
  and Firearms (BATF),
  12–13

California, 91
Canada

gun ownership in
  extent of, 29
  violence and, 88
  handgun murders in, 91
Carter, Gregg Lee
  on effects of culture of
    violence, 87
  on Handgun Control, Inc.,
    19
  on need for guns in colonial
    America, 45
Castano Group, 76
Caywood, Susan, 81
Center to Prevent Handgun
  Violence, 33
Chicago, Illinois, 70
Chicago Tribune (newspaper),
  71
children. *See* minors
Christoffel, Kathy Kauffer,
  35
civil rights movement, 13
Clinton, Bill
  on changing cultures, 94
  on gun registration, 57
Clinton, Hillary, 92
Coalition to Stop Gun
  Violence, 24
Colt six-shooters, 11
concealed weapons, 25,
  28–29
Constitution
  Bill of Rights and, 10, 49

Eighteenth Amendment of, 11–12
Second Amendment of
  reasons for, 10, 43–44
  rulings on, 12
    Supreme Court, 51–52
  should be repealed, 53
  wording of, 10, 43, 49
cop-killer bullets, 14
courts, 12, 52
  see also Supreme Court
crimes, gun-related
  extent of, 55, 91
  concealed weapons and, 25, 28–29
  decreases with
    gun ownership, 26
    gun registration, 57
  penalties for, should be increased, 59–60
culture of violence
  history of, 85–87, 91–92
  reasons for, 88–89, 92

Daley, Richard M., 70
Davis, Joe, 81
dealers, 13–14
deaths, 91
  extent of, 22–23
    decreases in households with guns, 30
    increases in households with guns, 24
Derringer, 10–11
Diaz, Tom
  on cost of gun violence, 72

on increasing lethalness of guns, 71
disabilities, 22
Douglas, William O., 49

education, 80–81, 83–84
England
  gun-murder rate in, 23
  handgun murders in, 91
  restrictions on guns in, 93

Farmer v. Higgins, 52
Federal Firearms Act, 13
felons
  guns and
    prosecution of, 61, 64
    restrictions on ownership of, 13, 51
Finland, 29
Firearms Owners' Protection Act, 14
Florida, 25, 28–29
Forester, Paul, 81–82
Francis, Samuel
  on concealed weapons laws, 29
  on need for use of force, 30
Franklin, Benjamin, 47–48
frontier heritage, 10, 11, 86, 91–92

Gamble, Tom, 81
Gauthier, Wendell, 76
Germany, 91
Glock 9s, 57
Glock 17s, 15

Great Britain
  gun-murder rate in, 23
  handgun murders in, 91
  restrictions on guns in, 93
Greece, 88
Grose, Francis, 44–45
Gun Control Act, 13–14, 51
Gun-Free School Zone Act,
  15–16
guns
  accessories for, 58
  availability of increases
    violence, 22
  banned types of, 13, 14–15,
    16
  banning of
    in cities, 17
    is necessary, 57–58, 93–95
    would harm society, 80
    would reduce violence, 91
      con, 85
  control of
    history of, 9, 10
    see also laws
    public opinion on, 55–56
  culture of
    history of, 10–12, 85–87,
      91–92
    reasons for, 88–89, 92
  militias and
    current, 50
    history of, 44, 45, 50
  numbers of, 34
  ownership of
    extent of, 23–24, 34, 78, 85
    history of, 44–46
  increase in, 28
  is not protected by Second
    Amendment, 49
  is protected by Second
    Amendment, 43
  minimum age for, is
    necessary, 59
  protects citizens, 26, 46–47
  regulation of, 56–57
  restrictions on, 10, 13, 16,
    17, 51
  safety devices for, 58–59
  sale of
    annual, 75
    illegal, 62, 69

Hack, Sabine, 32–33
Handgun Control, Inc. (HCI),
  16, 18–19
Handgun Epidemic
  Lowering Plan, 35
handguns, 16
Harris, Eric, 41
Hass, Robert, 68–69
Hayes, Tom, 68
hobbyists, 82–84
Hollon, Eugene, 92
Holocaust, 46–47
Horgan, Denis
  on necessity of banning
    guns, 93, 95
  on necessity of repealing
    Second Amendment, 53
hunting, 32, 80–82, 94

injuries, 22, 91

International Journal of Epidemiology, 23
Interpol, 87–88
Israel, 29

Janofsky, Michael, 65
Japan
  handgun murders in, 91
  social homogeneity in, 88
Journal of American Medical Association, 34
junk guns, 57

Kellerman, Jonathan
  on children as killers, 38, 39
  on violence in American folklore, 86
Kelly, Randy, 59–60
Kennesaw, Georgia, 27
Kinkel, Kip, 39, 41
Klebold, Dylan, 41
Kleck, Gary, 27
Korean War, 23
KTW bullets, 14

LaGioia v. Morton Grove, Il., 52
LaPierre, Wayne R.
  on cost of lawsuits, 74
  on enforcement of laws, 62
  on Project Exile, 65
Law Enforcement Officers' Protection Act, 14
laws
  enforcement of
    is effective, 62–65

should be increased, 61
  federal, 12–16, 56
local
  on banning guns, 17
  requiring gun ownership, 27
  should be stricter, 55
  state, 16–17, 55
    concealed weapons and, 25
    lawsuits against manufacturers and, 77–78
    penalties for gun-related crimes and, 59–60
  Supreme Court and, 46
lawsuits. *See under* manufacturers
Leddy, Edward F., 17–18
Levinson, Sanford, 46
Lewis v. U.S., 51
Los Angeles Times (newspaper), 37
Lott, John R., Jr.
  on concealed-weapons laws, 29
  on guns reducing crime, 26–27

machine guns, 14
Magnum Force Lobby (Leddy), 17–18
Making a Killing: The Business of Guns in America (Diaz), 71
manufacturers
  annual production by, 67
  are responsible for gun violence, 67, 72
    con, 73

lawsuits against, 71
  advertisements and, 68
  are fair, 68
  are unfair, 73
  cost of, 73
  flooding of markets and, 70
  product liability and,
    70–71, 74
  regulation of dealers and,
    68–70, 75
  will make guns
    unaffordable, 77
  restrictions on, 13–14
McCollum, Bill, 61–62
media, 68, 92
mentally ill, 13
militias
  current, 50
  federal government and, 46,
    51
  history of, 44, 45, 50
Miller, Jack, 51
Minnesota, 59–60
minorities, 10–12, 22, 91
minors
  access to guns by, 32, 34–35
  are not responsible for
    violence, 40
  gun ownership by, 59
  murders and, 33
    restrictions on, 13
  suicides and, 33
  see also schools
Morton Grove, Illinois, 17,
  52
murders

by handguns, 91
by teenagers, 33
Youth Violence Strike Force
  and, 63

National Council to Control
  Handguns, 18
National Firearms Act,
  12–13, 51
National Guard, 50
National Rifle Association
  (NRA), 14, 17–18
Navegar, 68
New American (magazine), 45
New England Journal of
  Medicine, 24
New Orleans, Louisiana,
  70–71
Newsweek (magazine), 38
New York
  gun sales laws in, 55
  lawsuits against
    manufacturers and, 68–70
New York Times (newspaper),
  62, 64, 65, 74
New Zealand
  gun ownership in, 29
  handgun murders in, 91
Norway, 88

Omnibus Crime Control and
  Safe Streets Act, 13–14

Penelas, Alex, 72
Pennsylvania rifle, 10–11
Pierce, Neil R.

on manufacturers and safety
  devices, 70–71
on manufacturers flooding
  markets, 70
Polsby, Daniel D., 28
Powell, Lewis, 52–53
Prohibition, 11–12
Project Exile, 63–65

registration
  is an invasion of privacy, 75
  is impractical, 75
  is necessary, 57
Revolutionary War, 43–44
Roaring Twenties, 11–12

safety devices, 58–59, 70–71
Saturday night specials, 14,
  57
Schiller, David, 64
schools
  guns in
    extent of, 32
    prosecution for, 61
  guns near, 15–16
  killings in
    described, 31, 34
    extent of, 37, 38
  violence in
    is caused by guns, 31
    con, 37
    Youth Violence Strike Force
      and, 63
shooting sports, competitive,
  83–84
Silko, Leslie Marmon, 80–81

Smith, Helen, 39–40
Smith & Wesson, 68
Southwick, Lawrence, 27–28
Spokesman-Review
  (newspaper), 73
Sugarman, Josh, 19
suicides, 24, 33, 91
Supreme Court
  described, 49
  Lewis v. U.S. and, 51
  states' rights and, 15–16, 46
  U.S. v. Miller and, 51
Switzerland, 29

Tantalus Syndrome, 89
TEC 9s, 57, 68
teenagers. *See* minors
Tefethan, James B., 10
Teflon bullets, 14
Teret, Stephen
  on public desire for stricter
    gun control laws, 55–56
  on safety devices, 58
Tiananmen Square, 47
Tice, D.J.
  on impropriety of lawsuits
    against manufacturers,
    77–78
  on need to uphold
    Constitution, 48
Toogood, Brian, 89
Tracinski, Robert W.,
  75–76
trigger locks, 58

Undetectable Firearms Act,
  14–15

U.S. v. Miller, 51
U.S. v. Warin, 52

Vietnam War, 23
Violence Policy Center, 19
Violent Crime Control and
 Law Enforcement Act, 16
Virginia, 55
Volk, Oleg, 82, 83, 84

waiting periods, 56–57
Walker, Bob, 59
Wall Street Journal
 (newspaper), 72
Washington Post (newspaper),
 64
Weir, William
 on gun culture, 88–89
 on Teflon bullets, 14
Well-Regulated Militia, A
 (Weir), 14, 88–89
Westervelt, Eric, 9
Wild West, 10, 11, 86,
 91–92
Wimershoff-Caplan, M., 47
Winchester rifles, 11
women, 27–28

Youth Violence Strike Force,
 63

About the Author

Terry O'Neill has a master's degree in American studies and taught high school English and social studies for more than a dozen years. She was an editor for Greenhaven's Opposing Viewpoints, American History, and Great Mysteries series and has both edited and written many other books and magazine articles on subjects ranging from biomedical ethics and adoption rights to ghosts and UFOs. She is the editor of a national trade magazine.